Safari Guide to the
Mammals of Eastern and Central Africa

STEVE SHELLEY

An identification guide covering Kenya, Tanzania, Uganda, eastern Zaïre, Rwanda, Zambia and Malaŵi.

Drawings and photographs by the author with a Foreword by Dr Perez M. Olindo, former Director, Department of Wildlife Conservation and Management, Kenya

MACMILLAN
PUBLISHERS

Copyright Text and Illustrations © Steve Shelley 1989

All rights reserved. No reproduction, copy or transmission
of this publication may be made without written permission.
No paragraph of this publication may be reproduced, copied
or transmitted save with written permission or in accordance
with the provisions of the Copyright Act 1956 (as amended).
Any person who does any unauthorised act in relation to
this publication may be liable to criminal prosecution and
civil claims for damages.

First published 1989

Published by *Macmillan Publishers Ltd*
London and Basingstoke
*Associated companies and representatives in Accra,
Auckland, Delhi, Dublin, Gaborone, Hamburg, Harare,
Hong Kong, Kuala Lumpur, Lagos, Manzini, Melbourne,
Mexico City, Nairobi, New York, Singapore, Tokyo.*

ISBN 0-333-49491-1

British Library Cataloguing in Publication Data
Shelley, Steve
  Safari guide to the mammals of East and Central Africa.
  1. Central Africa & East Africa. Mammals
  I. Title
  599'0967

ISBN 0-333-49491-1

With special thanks to Kay
for her ideas, support and tolerance through
many long days both on safari and at
the word processor.

Contents

Foreword	vi

PART 1 GOING ON SAFARI — 1

1.1	Introduction	2
1.2	East African habitats	5
1.3	The major national parks and reserves of East Africa	12
1.4	Wildlife conservation in East Africa	22
1.5	Wildlife photography	25
1.6	Watching wildlife	53
1.7	Close encounters in the bush	58
1.8	Some fascinating facts and further reading	62
1.9	Classification of mammals	65
1.10	Checklist of species	73

PART 2 THE MAMMALS — 77

2.1 UNGULATES

Buffalo and Antelopes

Buffalo	78		Impala	101
Eland	79		Gerenuk	102
Derby's eland	79		Grant's gazelle	103
Greater kudu	80		Thomson's gazelle	104
Lesser kudu	81		Klipspringer	105
Bongo	82		Oribi	106
Nyala	83		Steenbok	107
Sitatunga	84		Sharpe's grysbok	108
Bushbuck	85		Kirk's dikdik	109
Roan antelope	86		Guenther's dikdik	109
Sable antelople	87		Suni	110
Fringe eared oryx	88		Pigmy antelope	110
Beisa oryx	88		Yellow backed duiker	111
Wildebeest	89		Abbot's duiker	112
Coke's hartebeest	90		Common duiker	113
Jackson's hartebeest	90		Peter's duiker	114
Lichtenstein's hartebeest	91		Black fronted duiker	115
Topi	92		White bellied duiker	116
Tsessebe	92		Bay duiker	116
Hirola	93		Red duiker	117
Common waterbuck	94		Ruwenzori red duiker	117
Defassa waterbuck	94		Natal red duiker	117
Lechwe	95		Red flanked duiker	118
Puku	96		Zanzibar duiker	119
Uganda kob	97		Blue duiker	120
Bohor reedbuck	98		**Pigs**	
Mountain reedbuck	99		Giant forest hog	121
Southern reedbuck	100		Warthog	122
			Bushpig	123

Hippopotamus
Hippopotamus — 124

Giraffe
Common giraffe — 125
Reticulated giraffe — 126
Okapi — 127

Zebra
Grevy's zebra — 128
Common zebra — 129

Rhinoceros
White rhinoceros — 130
Black rhinoceros — 131

2.2 ELEPHANT
African elephant — 133

2.3 CARNIVORES
Hyenas
Spotted hyena — 134
Striped hyena — 135
Aardwolf — 136

Dogs, Jackals and Foxes
Wild dog — 137
Black backed jackal — 138
Side striped jackal — 139
Golden jackal — 140
Bat eared fox — 141

Cats and Cat-like Mammals
Lion — 142
Leopard — 143
Cheetah — 144
Serval — 145
Caracal — 146
Golden cat — 147
African wild cat — 148
African civet — 149
Tree civet — 150
Large spotted genet — 151
Small spotted genet — 151

Mongooses
White tailed mongoose — 152
Large grey mongoose — 153
Marsh mongoose — 154
Meller's mongoose — 155
Selous' mongoose — 156
Bushy tailed mongoose — 157
Slender mongoose — 158
Banded mongoose — 159
Dwarf mongoose — 160

Otters, Badgers and Weasels
Clawless otter — 161
Spotted necked otter — 161
Honey badger — 162
Striped polecat — 163
Striped weasel — 163

2.4 PRIMATES
Apes
Mountain gorilla — 164
Eastern lowland gorilla — 164
Chimpanzee — 165

Monkeys
Olive baboon — 166
Yellow baboon — 166
Chacma baboon — 166
Sykes' monkey — 167
Blue monkey — 167
Golden monkey — 167
L'Hoest's monkey — 167
De Brazza's monkey — 168
White nosed monkey — 169
Vervet monkey — 170
Patas monkey — 171
Black and white colobus — 172
Red colobus — 173
Black mangabey — 174

Bushbabies
Potto — 175
Thick tailed bushbaby — 176
Lesser bushbaby — 177
Demidoff's bushbaby — 177

2.5 OTHER MAMMALS
Aardvark — 178
Pangolin — 179
Porcupine — 180
Greater canerat — 181
Lesser canerat — 181
Ground squirrel — 182
Springhare — 183
African hare — 184
Scrub hare — 184
Bunyoro rabbit — 185
Red rock rabbit — 185
Rock hyrax — 186
Tree hyrax — 187
Hedgehog — 188

Master index to species — 189

Foreword

There are many guidebooks to the wildlife of East Africa, covering national parks, reserves and popular tourist sites, but until now no single volume has exclusively devoted such complete attention to the mammals of this region as the *Safari Guide to the Mammals of East and Central Africa* has succeeded in accomplishing.

This *Safari Guide* is expertly produced and can be readily used by scholars, university students and high school pupils as well as by tourists. The *Guide* can also be used as a reference book by Governments concerned in determining quickly and accurately the field status of those species covered.

At the time of going to press, the ranges inhabited by certain species have been further reduced by the conversion of natural habitats into arable land for human food production. The *Guide* may therefore serve another useful purpose in bringing to light the fact that hard decisions need to be made by the various States to enter into active partnerships with land owners who accommodate large numbers of the mammals the reader will be introduced to in this *Guide*. Otherwise, the National Parks and Reserves which today may provide adequate sanctuary will soon remain but islands in a sea of humanity.

We have seen time and again visitors to our country who amass impressive collections of the photographs they have taken — but how much less would a first-time visitor know about these beautiful animals without the type of explanatory notes and illustrations that have been assembled here for easy reference?

The *Safari Guide* further contributes to the conservation of these mammals by providing information on how their habits and behaviour affect future survival. Those of us who are actively involved in managing and conserving Africa's wildlife hope that everyone who reads this book will learn a little more, not just about the mammals themselves but also about the problems and opportunities we face in preserving them for the future. By taking the trouble to understand the relationships between wild animals, their habitats and human development, visitors to our national parks and reserves will find their safaris more interesting and rewarding. It is my hope that every such visitor will be able to play his or her part in promoting our conservation message.

For those who wish to know better the animals around them, this *Safari Guide* is highly recommended. For students, it is an easy source of reference and for the tourist, it is a fine souvenir to enrich the memories of a safari.

The *Safari Guide to the Mammals of East and Central Africa* is recommended to all without reservation or hesitation.

Dr Perez M. Olindo
former Director
Department of Wildlife Conservation and Management
Kenya

PART 1
Going on Safari

1.1 Introduction

So often on safari, someone asks the question 'What animal is that?'. Back comes the answer, 'Oh, it's just another buck.' Or, 'It's a deer.'

Just another buck? There are more than fifty species of buck in East Africa, 'buck' being a colloquial term for antelope, one of the most prolific and successful groups of animals on earth. Deer? There are no deer at all to be found in tropical Africa.

At first sight, the variety of mammals that can be seen throughout the parks and reserves of the eastern part of the African continent is bewildering and incredible. Yet more and more people are becoming interested in our fast disappearing wildlife, joining conservation groups and nature societies and, whenever they get the chance, going 'on safari'. This book has been produced for those people. It is designed to provide a name and basic behavioural information about 'that buck' – as well as the carnivores, primates, rodents and other animals that you may encounter on safari in East Africa.

The illustrations are made largely from my own photographs. Particular distinguishing features of each species are marked with short line indicators as is modern practice in many field guides.

The accompanying notes are based on observations from eight years of African safaris, augmented by reference to a number of published works which are listed in the bibliography. But there are few hard and fast rules when we are observing the natural world and it is entirely possible that you might see some species where they are 'supposed' not to occur, or indulging in behaviour that they are 'supposed' not to do. One of the exciting things about being on safari is to observe something that seems to conflict with what the books say. There is scope for everyone to notice something new. Everyone's personal observations will be different.

The region called East Africa consists traditionally of Uganda, Kenya and Tanzania, the latter two countries certainly receiving the greatest numbers of safari visitors. However, people are becoming more adventurous and reserves in Malawi, Zambia and even Rwanda and eastern Zaïre are nowadays on many itineraries. I have included these countries within the area covered by this book but have drawn a line at the Zambezi River since there are other books which cover countries further south.

This book contains virtually all of the species occurring within this region but there may be certain minor omissions, especially from the forested parts of Zaïre which are ecologically more typical of central and western Africa. For example, there are species of bushbaby and monkey that occur in the forest here, but are unlikely to be seen except by the most dedicated researcher. Somewhat arbitrarily, I have not included some smaller mammals such as bats, rats, mice and tree squirrels. The intention has been to make this a practical book, of use to the greatest number of people.

The species have been grouped within families according to size and visual similarity. This means that they do not always follow strict zoological classification. Each species is, however, labelled with its taxonomic order and family in addition to the specific name in English and Latin. I hope thereby to have achieved a satisfactory compromise between scholarship and practicality. Where possible, each species is also labelled with its common name in Kiswahili (K), French (F), and German (D).

It should be mentioned that there is some disagreement between zoologists on the names and classification of certain species and sub-species. I have tried to present a balanced view consistent with the latest thinking.

Within each section, the general arrangement is for larger species to come first, progressing through related species to the smaller ones. Thus the buffalo and ponderous eland are first among the 'buck', with the diminutive 30 cm blue duiker last. The data given on size and weight are average figures and where the length is given, this includes the tail. There is often considerable variation between sexes and within the species in size as well as colouring. Often the male of a species is significantly larger than the female but this is not always so.

The spoor shown is usually the forefoot. Often, this is slightly larger than the hind foot, in order to support the extra weight of the forequarters. Where only the hind foot contacts the ground, as with the springhare for example, then this is the one that is shown. The dimensions given are of a typical length of the imprint on the ground.

The distribution maps give an overall idea of the range of each species but there will almost certainly be areas within these ranges where it does not occur, due to habitat specialisation, rarity and human development

Also included are a few hints on wildlife photography. There is nothing more distressing than to return from a long-planned safari with pictures that do not live up to the memories. There are some tips on finding and watching wildlife, some notes on conservation and a few anecdotes to whet the appetite.

East Africa possesses what must be the most varied range of habitats on earth. From coral reefs and mangrove swamps to glaciers and snowfields, there is just about every type of habitat imaginable. This is what makes the region so attractive and so interesting from many points of view. But it is alarming how quickly changes in habitat are taking place and, because of these changes the numbers and distribution of wild animals are changing too.

Looking at the distribution maps and comparing them with those of a few years ago, it is sad to see as blank areas the great open spaces that once teemed with wild creatures. For example, it is unusual nowadays to see cheetah in Kenya outside certain protected areas. In many areas, even the parks and reserves have failed to protect their wild inhabitants. Human development is often a cause, especially as some African countries have such high rates of population growth, but poaching also continues to be a major problem.

As the manuscript of this book was being completed, the results emerged of the latest elephant census in the Tsavo National Park complex. The alarming news is that elephant have been decimated even **within** the national park. Since the last count in 1973, elephant have been exterminated to such an extent that there are now only 15% of the numbers that existed then. And this is in a region heavily visited by tourists and supposedly well guarded by conservation authorities.

The rhino is another classic tale of wildlife woe. It has been poached to extinction in some countries, to the brink in others and is only really holding its own in certain reserves in southern Africa. Lion have been shot out of populated areas. Wild dog have succumbed to canine diseases, cheetah to pressure on their huge hunting terrains and bongo to excessive deforestation.

Many governments have realised the value of setting aside areas for the preservation of wildlife, not only for posterity but for shorter term gain through tourist revenues. If much wildlife is to survive in the face of a burgeoning human population, such areas are vital – and the bigger, the better. Too often, protected areas have later been deproclaimed. Others have been defeated in their purpose through the erection of fences across ancient migration routes. Now there is an additional fear that too many tourists may begin to destroy the beauty of what they have come to see.

There is a vogue for suggesting that wildlife should pay its way if it is to be allowed to survive. Tourism, hunting, rearing for meat: these are some of the possibilities. This view may be pragmatic but it is also a little arrogant. When you watch a herd of elephant drinking and bathing in the Uaso Ngiro river, a string of wildebeest plodding over the Serengeti plains, or a fish eagle soaring above the hippo in Lake Malaŵi, you can see that there is an artistry about wildlife that should need no justification to preserve.

Time after time people gaze at such sights with expressions on their faces that say, 'In spite of everything we read and hear, all is well with the world.' It is a tremendously comforting thought in these turbulent times.

To go 'on safari' offers such a refreshing view of the world that people can return renewed and invigorated, ready to face the routine of their lives with enthusiasm. It is surely no accident that many painters, poets, musicians, writers and philosophers have gained much of their inspiration from the wilderness and its wild inhabitants.

In a very real sense we need wildlife. After all the slaughter that has taken place in the name of settlement, agriculture and health, it is ironic that we humans so desperately need wilderness and wildlife simply to support our own psychic well-being. To reassure us that the world is not entirely how we have created it.

This book is dedicated to the wild animals of Africa. Let people preserve them not for gain alone but for their own sakes.

1.2 East African habitats

The diversity of habitats in Eastern Africa makes the region especially interesting from a biological and zoological point of view. This variety is a result of tremendous differences in altitude and rainfall patterns which give rise to a similarly broad diversity of mammals as well as other kinds of wildlife. For the visitor to East Africa, a great deal of interest can be added to a safari by including in the itinerary a range of habitats and ecological zones. Often, quite different scenery and wildlife will be seen.

Leaving aside the coral reefs and sea shores, which are themselves fascinating, there are three main categories of habitat within the region.

The **arid** zones include a number of desert, semi-desert and thornbush habitats.

Savanna zones cover a variety of grasslands and woodland types.

Where there is higher rainfall or other available moisture, **forests** of differing types occur.

These basic zones can be usefully split into a number of more descriptive categories but it is important to note that although these zones may change abruptly from one type to another, they also overlap and grade into one another. Mammal species are sometimes closely associated with a particular habitat while others occur more commonly at the ecotone or boundary between adjacent habitats.

Semi-desert

Although there are expanses devoid of vegetation, there are no true deserts in East Africa. Salt flats and lava fields occur which are colonised only by the hardiest of plants. These are especially noticeable in northern Kenya where rainfall is very low. There are huge plains of blackened lava boulders that absorb heat and raise temperatures well beyond any comfort level. But even throughout the arid Northern Frontier District, there is a sparse covering of grasses, succulents and shrubs on a sandy substrate that is typically semi-desert. Rainfall in these areas is variable and runs off in well defined courses or luggas and a stronger growth of larger shrubs and trees occurs along these.

Typical plant species of these arid regions are disperma, aloe, calotropis, sanseveria, balanites and euphorbia. Such regions are also often characterised by tall columns of termite mounds. Typical mammal species of these areas include oryx, dikdik, gerenuk, reticulated giraffe and Grevy's zebra. Semi-desert reserves of the region are Sibiloi, Samburu and Shaba.

Bush thicket

Arid zones grade into areas of greater plant density. Where there is higher rainfall or run-off in the form of seasonal streams, a tangled growth of thorny bushes may occur. This is variously described as bushland, thicket, nyika or thornbush scrub. Within East Africa, this type of habitat occurs typically at altitudes less than 3000' (1000 m). Throughout the dry season, the vegetation in these zones is bare and seems almost to be dead. Only when the rains come is there a frantic sprouting of flowers and leaves. The hardpan floor of thicket regions may be rather impervious to water and in places permanent or semi-permanent waterholes form that attract all kinds of wildlife.

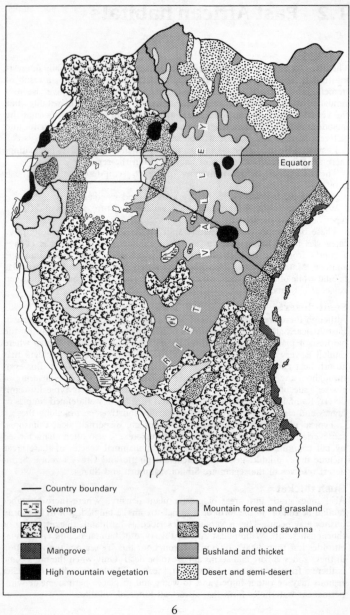

Plant species here include commiphora, combretum, acacia and lannia. These may grow into trees as high as 15 – 20′ (5 – 6 m). In some areas of thornbush, where it begins to merge into woodland, baobab trees occur. These strange but peculiarly beautiful trees provide a reservoir of moisture within their bark that attracts many mammals, birds, reptiles and insects.

In spite of seeming a rather harsh environment, bush thicket is a habitat in which a wide variety of mammals may be found. In the thornier areas, dikdik, gerenuk and lesser kudu occur. Larger species include rhinoceros and elephant while closer to watercourses there may be impala, giraffe, lion and leopard. Rhinos and elephant play an important role in clearing passages through this vegetation and where these species have been eliminated, grassland may revert to scrub. Reserves in which thornbush occurs include Meru, Kora, Tsavo, Tarangire, Ruaha and many others.

Savanna

This is a much over-used word that describes a variety of grassy and wooded habitats. It is generally associated with the typical plains of East Africa where vast stretches of grassland support an enormous mass of antelopes and other mammal species. There may be a very clear cut line between grassland and woodland or thornbush. This is often the result of fire which destroys small saplings and prevents the growth of shrubs and trees but which cannot gain a hold on established trees. Many pastoral tribes throughout Africa deliberately burn grasslands before the rains to encourage a faster resurgence of green shoots. Grasses have evolved to withstand such pressures and apparently completely burnt out areas soon regenerate a covering of grass. If the rains are late, however, this practice of burning can destroy what little grazing remained.

In many areas, shrubs and trees intrude into grassland giving an intermediate mixed habitat. Various kinds of acacia, often called thorn trees, are typical of this sort of zone. The flat topped umbrella tree, *Acacia tortilis*, and the yellow barked fever tree, *Acacia xanthophloea*, are two of the region's most typical and attractive savanna trees. The latter is particularly associated with watercourses where the presence of mosquitoes and other insects gave rise to its common name.

Even amongst grasslands, there are various kinds, characterised by the type of soil, drainage and grass species supported. One of the most common grasses is red oat grass, *Themeda triandra*. When it is fully grown and seen in a late afternoon light, plains of this grass have a glorious red gold colouring.

The East African grassland savannas support a vast number of grazing mammals including wildebeest, hartebeest, zebra and gazelles. Other typical species include lion, cheetah, hyena, jackals and bat eared fox. Crossing the savanna to reach thickets or woodlands may be giraffe, elephant and rhinoceros.

The famous savanna reserves of the region include Mara, Serengeti, Ngorongoro, Ruwenzori and Nyika Plateau. Many other reserves contain grasslands of various types.

Woodland

Some kinds of savanna grade into woodland in such a way that there is little clear demarcation between the different zones. A higher level of rainfall is usually necessary to support a growth of trees but woodlands are generally dry when compared with tropical forests or temperate woodlands. Tree species are generally deciduous, varying from acacias in drier areas to taller combretum, brachystegia and terminalia species where the water table is higher.

Woodland is especially common in the southern part of the region where the so-called miombo woodland covers much of southern Tanzania, Malaŵi and Zambia. This kind of habitat occurs largely between 2000' and 6000' (600 – 1800 m) above sea-level with the dominant tree species varying according to altitude and rainfall. Brachystegia species tend to be the most common throughout this zone. Further south, towards the Zambezi river and Kalahari sands, these tree species are gradually replaced by mopane. These trees show remarkable colouring at certain seasons with old bronze, golden yellow and fresh green leaves present at the same time.

As a wildlife habitat, woodlands can seem rather sterile and uninteresting, especially as the miombo zone stretches uninterrupted and unchanging for thousands of miles in a broad belt across the continent. However, it supports a range of mammal species, some of which are very closely associated with this habitat. These species include roan and sable antelope, Lichtenstein's hartebeest and greater kudu. In river valleys there may be puku, reedbuck, buffalo and elephant together with predators such as lion and leopard. Rocky ridges and koppies may be home to klipspringer. In the tangled woodlands of southern Malaŵi, nyala occur.

Woodland reserves of the region include Ruaha, Selous, Luangwa, Kafue and Lengwe. Many other parks and reserves contain areas of woodland of various sorts.

Forest

The tropical rain forest of central Africa is only one of several different kinds of forest. Forests occur in areas of high rainfall or where water is available in other ways. Thus there are montane forests nurtured by both rainfall and mists, riverine or gallery forests along the courses of rivers and mangrove forests along the sea shore. Groundwater forests exist on wetland margins, for example in Lake Manyara.

The common factor in all tropical forests is an incredible diversity of tree species some of which reach heights over 150' (45m). These form a canopy below which a number of other levels occur often with a tangled growth of shrubs and creepers at ground level. Lowland rain forest occurs in the region throughout much of eastern Zaïre as well parts of western Uganda, Rwanda and Tanzania. Typical mammal species of this zone are the okapi, bongo, giant forest hog and many of the duikers. Montane forests occur above 8000' (2500 m) on the massifs of the region. These include the Ruwenzoris on the Uganda, Zaïre, Rwanda boundaries, the Cheranganis, Mau, Aberdares and Mt Kenya in Kenya and Mt Kilimanjaro, the Usambaras and Ulungurus in Tanzania. Bongo, buffalo, elephant and duiker species may be common in these forests.

Riverine forests occur along many waterways, even seasonal streams. These forests may be very narrow, confined to the river banks, or rather wider. In otherwise dry areas, such forests may contain palms of various species. The Uaso Ngiro river in Samburu and Shaba is a good example of this. Mammal species here may be similar to other forest areas but many other woodland or savanna species pass through these forests to reach water. Some trees such as the doum and borassus palms produce seeds in the form of very hard nuts. These have evolved to withstand drought, fire and being eaten by elephants. They may have difficulty in germinating unless they are burnt or partially digested.

Forest reserves of the region include Kahuzi-Biega in Zaïre, Gombe, Kilimanjaro and Arusha in Tanzania, Volcanoes in Rwanda, Ruwenzori in Uganda and Aberdares and Mt Kenya in Kenya. The Tana River Primate Reserve in north east Kenya covers a patch of riverine forest. Other examples of riverine forests can be found in the Mara and Serengeti.

Wetlands

This is an all-encompassing word to describe lakeshores, swamps, river deltas and floodplains. These areas combine aquatic and terrestrial characteristics. In open water, plants such as papyrus, bulrushes and water lilies may occur. At the edges, various reeds, sedges and rank grasses grow. Floating plants form masses that take on a terrestrial nature. Wetlands can be a very rich habitat for many kinds of animal life and can be very beautiful. They are, however, difficult to penetrate. Mammal species include hippopotamus, waterbuck, reedbuck, canerat, puku, lechwe, buffalo and elephant.

Wetlands reserves include Lake Nakuru, Saiwa Swamp, Akagera, Ruwenzori, Katavi and parts of Luangwa and Kafue.

Afro-alpine zone

On the high mountains of the region such as the Ruwenzoris, Aberdares, Mt Kenya and Mt Kilimanjaro, the vegetation changes in clearly defined bands according to altitude. Above the forests at around 9000' (2750 m), a zone of dense bamboo forest occurs. Although a kind of grass, bamboo may grow to a height of 30' (10 m) and it forms a dense mass of stems that is very difficult to pass through. This habitat may contain buffalo, elephant or bongo but little else.

Above this belt there is often an area of tall hagenia trees interspersed with grassy clearings. This grades into a zone of giant heathers that grow to 15' (5 m) or more. Beyond this, at altitudes over 10 000' (3000 m), boggy moorlands exist with a dense covering of grasses and sedges. Mammals may occur in these areas, especially in the dry seasons. These may include elephant, buffalo, duikers, leopard and serval.

Since these zones lie very close to the equator, the intensity of sunlight is very great. Coupled with a high moisture level, this has given rise to some freak plant species such as giant groundsels and lobelias which form tall flower spikes many feet longer than their lowland relatives.

Ecology

The study of the relationships of wild animals both with each other and the habitat in which they live is called ecology. Through observing the types of habitat as well as the animals themselves, some revealing insights can be gained into the habits and distribution of both wildlife and humans. The variations in vegetation throughout East Africa are as fascinating as the variations in other forms of wildlife and in the scenery itself and it is quickly possible to note particular associations.

It is tragic that some of these habitats, especially forests and wetlands, are being destroyed in pursuit of a short term economic gain. Destruction of forests is already causing a change in rainfall patterns and in the absorption and run-off of water and this is likely to have drastic long-term effects upon agriculture in East Africa.

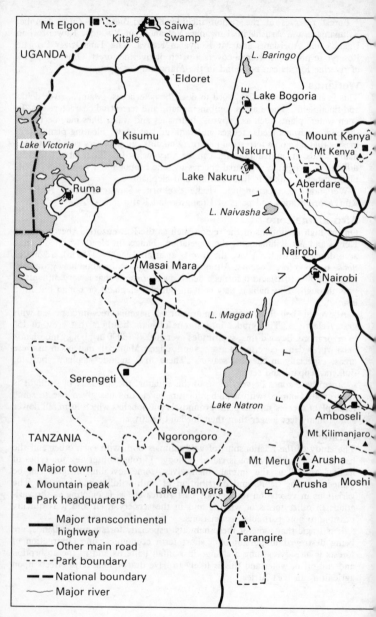

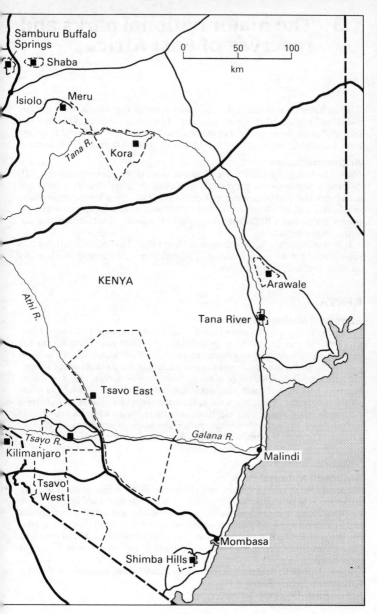

1.3 The major national parks and reserves of East Africa

This includes all national parks and game reserves that are either commonly visited or have special importance for particular species. It is not an exhaustive listing of every protected area of the region. The mammals referred to do not form a complete list either but are species of special interest in that area.

Accommodation
Note: The lodges listed are those within or close to the park boundaries. Self-catering accommodation means that you need to bring your own food and sometimes also bedding, water and everything else. Very few campsites have any facilities at all. Water, food and fuel should always be carried and even nearby towns and villages may not provide the shops or restaurants that the visitor might expect.

It is also important to note that camps and lodges have become run down in some places and are newly installed in others, so it is advisable to check locally on their availability or existence.

KENYA

Aberdare National Park
225 sq ml (585 sq km) of forested foothills and mountain moorlands from 6000' to 13000' in altitude (1830 m to 4000 m). The park lies very close to the equator but the undulating plateau at around 10 000' which forms the main part of the park has regular night frosts. Including the foothills of the salient, the park contains a wide range of forest types such as riverine and mist forest, bamboo, hagenia and giant heathers. Giant groundsel and giant lobelia occur on the mountains. There are some spectacular waterfalls. The salient contains bushbuck, giant forest hog, elephant, rhino and bongo while the moorlands are inhabited by buffalo, common duiker and black or melanistic serval.
Lodges: The Ark, Treetops, Outspan, Aberdare Country Club
Self-catering: Kiandogoro Fishing Camp
Campsites: Available

Amboseli National Park
148 sq ml (385 sq km) of flat savanna at the foot of Mt Kilimanjaro. The main attraction is a perennial swamp which attracts both mammals and extensive birdlife. There is a patch of forest, some woodland and areas of open plains and thornbush scrub. Dry season concentrations of plains game are spectacular. Big herds of elephant are often present and a few black rhino exist in the park. Cheetah are often seen here. There are also heavy concentrations of tourists at most seasons.
Lodges: Amboseli, Amboseli Serena, Gona Safari Camp, Kilimanjaro Buffalo, Kilimanjaro Safari, Kimana
Self-catering: Ol Tukai
Campsites: Available

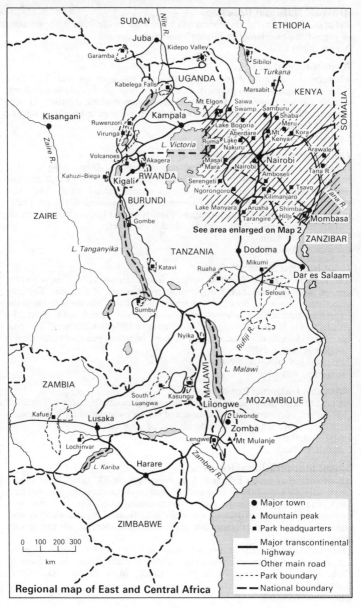

Arawale National Reserve
204 sq ml (530 sq km) of arid thornbush scrub close to the Tana River set aside to protect the rare hirola or Hunter's hartebeest.
No overnight facilities

Kora National Reserve
691 sq ml (1790 sq km) of arid thornbush scrub and open savanna. The Tana River forms the reserve's northern boundary. Previously heavily poached and animals are not numerous. Lesser kudu are common along the river. George Adamson has brought a measure of recognition to the area and has reintroduced lion and leopard.
Campsites: Available

Lake Bogoria National Reserve
A small reserve at 42 sq ml (110 sq km) consisting of a soda lake lying in a cleft in the hills within the Rift Valley. There is a patch of forest as well as some acacia woodland and the hillsides are clad with thornbush scrub. The main attraction is the huge numbers of flamingoes but it is also one of the few places in Kenya where there is much chance of seeing greater kudu. Other mammals include klipspringer, Grant's gazelle, dikdik and civet.
Lodges: To be built
Campsites: Available

Lake Nakuru National Park
The 77 sq ml (200 sq km) of this park encircle a large soda lake and cover an area of woodland and thornbush savanna to the south of the lake. The lake sometimes attracts big flocks of flamingoes and pelicans but the area has some interesting mammals. These include bohor reedbuck, introduced Rothschild's giraffe, leopard, wild cat and some huge herds of Defassa waterbuck. The lake has suffered some dramatic changes of level in recent years and was almost completely dry in 1988.
Lodges: Lion Hill, Lake Nakuru
Campsites: Available

Marsabit National Reserve
An area of semi-desert surrounding a forest-clad mountain. Area is 810 sq ml (2090 sq km). Greater kudu occur here and the area was famed for large tusked elephants. Other mammals include reticulated giraffe.
Lodges: Marsabit
Campsites: Available

Masai Mara National Reserve
An area of rolling grassy hills and plains covering some 645 sq ml (1670 sq km). Other habitats within the reserve include woodland, thornbush scrub, riverine forest and swamps. A large variety of mammals occur here with lion and migrating wildebeest providing the main attractions. Leopard, cheetah and rhino are often seen and there are always large numbers of tourists in this popular reserve.
Lodges and tented camps: Cottar's Camp, Fig Tree Camp, Governor's Camp, Little Governor's, Kichwa Tembo Camp, Mara Buffalo Camp, Mara Intrepids Club, Mara River Camp, Mara Sarova Camp, Mara Serena, Mara Sopa, Keekorok
Campsites: Available

Meru National Park
336 sq ml (870 sq km) of thornbush scrub and grassy plains. There is an extensive swamp and woodland along several rivers including the Tana. The area is well watered but in an arid zone. The park straddles the equator. Northern species such as reticulated giraffe and Grevy's zebra are here at their southernmost limits. Gerenuk are common and many other species can be seen. A small herd of introduced white rhino was destroyed by poachers in late 1988.
Lodge: Meru Mulika
Self-catering: Leopard Rock
Campsites: Available

Mt Elgon National Park
66 sq ml (170 sq km) of mountain forest and moorland on the Uganda border. Altitude ranges from 6000' to 14 000' (1800 m to 4250 m). Typical mountain species occur here including giant forest hog, elephant and duiker.
Lodge: Mt Elgon
Campsites: Available

Mt Kenya National Park
232 sq ml (600 sq km) of equatorial mountain forest and moorland from 10 000' to the peak at over 17 000' (3000 m to 5200 m). The mountain itself adds glaciers and snow fields to the list of habitats within the park. Buffalo, rhino and leopard occur on the mountain as well as a good variety of other mammals.
Lodges: Mountain Lodge, Mount Kenya Safari Club, Naro Moru River Lodge
Self-catering: Meru Mt Kenya Lodge (Chogoria), Mackinders Camp, Met Station, Mountain Club Huts
Campsites: Available

Nairobi National Park
46 sq ml (120 sq km) of rolling grassy plains on the edge of the city. Dry season concentrations of plains game are impressive and there is a large variety of mammals including lion, cheetah, black rhino, eland and kongoni. Leopard and bushbuck occur in the forest and hippo in the Mbgathi River. An underrated park of considerable interest.
No overnight facilities

Ruma National Park (previously Lambwe Valley)
75 sq ml (194 sq km) of thornbush and woodland close to Lake Victoria. The area is one of few in Kenya where roan antelope and oribi occur in any numbers.
Campsites: Available

Saiwa Swamp National Park
Not even a square mile in extent (1.9 sq km), this park has been established to protect the only group of sitatunga in Kenya. Other interesting mammals include De Brazza's monkey and the spotted necked otter.
Campsites: Available

Samburu National Reserve
Together with the contiguous Buffalo Springs reserve, Samburu covers an area of 216 sq ml (560 sq km) of arid thornbush scrub and semi-desert. It is bisected by the Uaso Ngiro River which supports a strip of forest and woodland. There are areas of grassy plains. Scenery is spectacular with the sugar-loaf shape of Ololokwe to the north and the glaciers of Mt Kenya visible to the south.

Reticulated giraffe, gerenuk and Grevy's zebra are common here as well as beisa oryx. A wide range of other species can be seen including elephant, dikdik, cheetah and leopard.
Lodges: Samburu, Samburu Serena, Buffalo Springs Camp, Larsen's Camp
Campsites: Available

Shaba National Reserve
93 sq ml (240 sq km) of arid thornbush along the Uaso Ngiro River east of Samburu. Animal life is not abundant but the area has magnificent wild scenery. Species include elephant, gerenuk, Grant's gazelle and oryx.
Lodges: Shaba Sarova Lodge
Campsites: Available

Shimba Hills National Reserve
73 sq ml (190 sq km) of rolling park-like hills just half an hour's drive from the coastal resorts of Diani. There is extensive forest in which walking trails can be followed. This is the only location in Kenya where sable antelope occur. Other species include roan antelope, elephant, blue monkey and black and white colobus.
Lodges: Shimba Hills
Campsites: Available

Sibiloi National Park
618 sq ml (1600 sq km) of desert on the eastern shore of Lake Turkana. Remote, hot, windy and dusty. Mammals include Grevy's zebra, Grant's gazelle, oryx and tiang (topi). The park is the site of important archeological excavations.
Campsites: Available

Tana River Primate Reserve
A small patch of riverine forest along the banks of the Tana River measuring 66 sq ml (170 sq km). It has been established to protect Kenya's only endemic species of monkeys, the Tana River crested mangabey, the Tana River red colobus and a subspecies of Sykes' monkey. During the dry season other mammals use the reserve for access to the river. These include elephant, lesser kudu, oryx, red duiker and many more.
Campsite: Available

Tsavo East National Park
5000 sq ml (13 000 sq km) of arid thornbush scrub intersected by the Galana River. A wide range of species in this vast area includes elephant, lion, gerenuk and lesser kudu. A large part of the park is not open to the general public.
Lodges: Voi Safari, Crocodile Camp, Tsavo Safari Camp
Self-catering: Aruba Lodge
Campsites: Available

Tsavo West National Park
3000 sq ml (7770 sq km) of plains, mountains and thornbush adjoining Tsavo East. The park includes Mzima Springs, a freshwater spring that feeds the Tsavo River and is home to large numbers of hippo. A very wide range of mammal species occurs within the park including lion, cheetah, elephant, kongoni, klipspringer and many, many more. Animals are sometimes difficult to find in this vast landscape but the scenery is spectacular.
Lodges: Kilaguni, Ngulia, Salt Lick, Taita Hills

Self-catering: Kitani Safari Camp, Ngulia Safari Camp
Campsites: Available

TANZANIA

Arusha National Park
This park includes an amazing variety of habitats from lakes and craters, through woodland and forests to high altitude mountain. Total area is 540 sq ml (1400 sq km) from 5000′ to the summit of Mt Meru at 14 979′ (1525 m to 4565 m). Each habitat contains different species. For example, red duiker can be found in the forest, giraffe in the woodland, waterbuck by the lakes and buffalo higher on the mountain.
Lodges: Momela Game; Mount Meru Game Sanctuary (at Usa River)
Campsites: Available

Gombe National Park
Woodland and forest on the shore of Lake Tanganyika. Area 200 sq ml (520 sq km). The park was established to protect the colony of chimpanzees but other mammals also occur.
Self-catering accommodation: Available

Lake Manyara National Park
123 sq ml (319 sq km) of lake and forest and savanna on its western shore. A wide range of mammals includes elephant, lion, hippo and many others. The Rift Valley escarpment forms the park's western boundary.
Lodges: Lake Manyara Hotel
Campsites: Available

Katavi National Park
298 sq ml (770 sq km) of lakes, swamps, savanna and woodlands. Amongst the many species occurring here are puku, roan and sable antelope and tsessebe at the northern extreme of its range.
Campsites: Available

Kilimanjaro National Park
298 sq ml (770 sq km) of mountain from 6000′ to the peak at 19 340′ (1830 m to 5895 m). The area includes rain forest, moorlands and bare rock and snow towards the top. Elephant, buffalo and leopard occur in the forest, eland on the moorlands. The rare Abbot's duiker is known only from the forest of this and neighbouring mountains.
Lodges: Marangu, Kibo
Self-catering accommodation and campsites: Available

Mikumi National Park
1247 sq ml (3230 sq km) of grassland, floodplain and riverine forest. Large numbers of elephant and buffalo occur here. Other species include Lichtenstein's hartebeest and sable antelope.
Lodges: Mikumi Wildlife Lodge, Mikumi Lodge
Campsites: Available

Ngorongoro Conservation Area
Over 2000 sq ml (5200 sq km) which includes the famous crater, 12 ml in diameter and 2000′ deep (19km, 600m). The crater contains grassland, a lake,

swamps and woodland. The remainder of the conservation area also includes mountain forest and lower level savanna. An enormous range of mammals occurs here including black rhino, lion, serval, hyena, golden jackal, cheetah, buffalo and many more.
Lodges: Ngorongoro Crater, Ngorongoro Safari, Ngorongoro, Lerai
Self-catering: Ngorongoro Forest Lodge
Campsites: Available

Ruaha National Park
A large park of wooded hills, grassy savanna, swamps and rivers covering over 5000sq ml (13 000 sq km). Large concentrations of animals occur along the Great Ruaha River. These include big herds of elephant and buffalo. Antelope include roan, sable, Lichtenstein's hartebeest and both greater and lesser kudu. Grant's gazelle is here close to the southern extreme of its range.
Self-catering accommodation and campsites: Available

Selous Game Reserve
An enormous area of 20 000 sq ml (51 800 sq km) astride the Rufiji and Great Ruaha Rivers. A wide range of habitats include grassland, thornbush, woodlands and forest. There are large herds of elephant and sable; roan and Lichtenstein's hartebeest occur here. The brindled gnu replaces the white bearded gnu from here southwards.
Tented camps and campsites: Available

Serengeti National Park
5700 sq ml (14 760 sq km) of mainly grassland savanna but also including woodlands, thornbush, koppies and riverine forest. The largest concentrations of plains game occur seasonally here including wildebeest, zebra, topi, kongoni and gazelle. Lion, cheetah and wild dog can be seen along with a huge range of other species.
Lodges: Seronera, Lobo
Tented camp: Ndutu
Campsites: Available

Tarangire National Park
Over 1000 sq ml (2600 sq km) of dry thornbush and woodland savanna. The Tarangire River provides a permanent water source and large dry season concentrations of game occur here. Amongst other species, lesser kudu, oryx and eland can be seen here.
Tented camp: Tarangire Safari Camp
Campsites: Available

MALAŴI

Kasungu National Park
800 sq ml (2072 sq km) of undulating woodland and grassy valleys containing a good variety of animal species. These include elephant, Lichtenstein's hartebeest, roan, sable and greater kudu as well as the usual predators.
Lodges: Lifupa
Campsites: Available

Lengwe National Park
A small park at 50 sq ml (130 sq km) which is largely low lying thornbush

scrub. The main attraction of the park is the nyala, here at its northernmost limit. Greater kudu also occur and blue monkeys may be seen. Wooden hides have been provided at certain waterholes.
Self-catering accommodation: Available

Liwonde National Park
A small but delightful woodland park stretching along several miles of the Shire River at the southern end of Lake Malawi. Animal species include lion, elephant, sable, greater kudu, common waterbuck and hippo.
Lodges: Kudya Discovery
Campsites: Available

Nyika National Park
The Nyika Plateau is some 6800' (2100m) above sea-level and 120 sq ml (310 sq km) of rolling grasslands constitutes the park. It is approached up a steep escarpment and has a real feeling of being another world, cut off from the rest of the country. The air is bracing and frost is possible in the middle of the year. There is a wide variety of wildlife on the plateau including eland, roan antelope, zebra, reedbuck and duiker.
Self-catering: Chilinda Camp

ZAMBIA

Lochinvar National Park
158 sq ml (410 sq km) of floodplains close to the Kafue River. The park was established to protect a large population of the Kafue lechwe. Other species include greater kudu, oribi, wildebeest and zebra.
Self-catering accommodation: Available

Kafue National Park
At 8550 sq ml (22150 sq km), Kafue is one of the largest parks in Africa, indeed in the world. Much of the park is forested but extensive wetlands exist in the north. The Kafue River forms the eastern boundary of part of the park. A very wide range of mammal species includes puku and lechwe.
Lodges: Chunga, Musungwa, Ngoma
Self-catering: Chunga Kafwala, Lufupa, Moshi, Nanzhila
Campsites: Available

South Luangwa National Park
3475 sq ml (9000 sq km) of woodland savanna in the Luangwa River valley. The river forms the eastern boundary of the park. Other undeveloped national parks exist further north along the river. The park is particularly famed for its large numbers of elephant but there is an enormous variety of other species. Black rhino still occur here and the darkly coloured Thornicroft's giraffe is restricted to the Luangwa valley.
Lodges: Chichele, Luamfwa, Lundwe Safari, Mfuwe, Chibembe
Tented camps: Mwamba, Chinzambo, Tundwa, Big Lagoon, Lion

Sumbu National Park
780 sq ml (2020 sq km) of wetland and savanna at the southern end of Lake Tanganyika.

Lodges: Kasaba Bay, Ndole Bay, Nkamba Bay
Campsites: Available

RWANDA

Akagera National Park
The park follows the Kagera River along the Uganda and Tanzania borders. It is some 1080 sq ml (2800 sq km) in extent and covers a range of habitats from lakes and papyrus swamps through grassland and thornbush savanna to woodland and hillsides. The mammal species are similarly varied and include sitatunga, oribi, topi and leopard amongst many others.
Lodge: Kayonza

Volcanoes National Park
This park of 579 sq ml (1500 sq km) covers an area of bamboo and hagenia forest on the slopes of the spectacular range of volcanoes that separate Rwanda and Zaïre. There are areas of moorland at higher levels. Altitude ranges from 8000' to nearly 15 000' (2400 m to 4500 m). The park was established to protect the small remaining numbers of mountain gorilla but other mammal species present include elephant, yellow backed duiker, red duiker and bushbuck.
Lodge: Available in Ruhengeri
Campsites: Available

UGANDA

Kabalega Falls National Park
Previously called Murchison Falls, this park covers 1483 sq ml (3840 sq km) of grassland savanna and forest bisected by the River Nile. Lion, hippo and Rothschild's giraffe occur here as well as elephant and kob but many species have been seriously depleted during the unrest of the last decades.
Lodges: Chobe, Karuma Falls, Paraa
Campsites: Available

Kidepo Valley National Park
Arid savanna and mountains covering some 525 sq ml (1360 sq km). A wide range of species includes greater and lesser kudu, Grant's gazelle, oribi and mountain reedbuck. Although protected by its remoteness from much of the poaching that has affected other Uganda parks, Kidepo has more recently suffered from its proximity to the unrest in neighbouring southern Sudan.
Campsites: Available

Ruwenzori National Park
770 sq ml (1994 sq km) of lakes, swamps, grasslands, forests and hills. Previously called the Queen Elizabeth National Park, it should not be confused with the nearby Ruwenzori Mountains, most of which lie outside the park boundaries. The lakes have undergone several changes of name and are still referred to locally as Lakes Edward and George. Mammals have been seriously depleted but are gradually returning. Elephant used to occur in the biggest herds in Africa but are now limited in number. Vast herds of hippo still occur in Lake Edward and other species include kob, topi and buffalo. Rather surprisingly, there seem to be no impala in what ought to be an ideal habitat.
Lodges: Mweya, Ishasha River
Campsites: Available

EASTERN ZAÏRE

Kahuzi-Biega National Park
This area of mountain rain forest covers some 2300 sq ml (6000 sq km) close to the Burundi and Rwanda borders. The main attraction is the eastern lowland gorilla but chimpanzee and other rare primates also occur here. Other mammals include elephant and various species of duiker.
Accommodation: Available in Bukavu
Campsites: Available

Virunga National Park
Over 3000 sq ml (7770 sq km) of lakes, swamps, grasslands, forests, mountains, moorlands and glaciers from the shores of Lake Edward to the peaks of the Ruwenzori Mountains. Altitude range is from 2500' to nearly 17 000' (800 m to over 5000 m). A similarly diverse range of mammals occurs here, heightened by the park's special position at the boundary between typical East African savanna and the Central African forest zone. Species include elephant, lion, topi, kob, mountain gorilla, chimpanzee and bongo, to name but a few.
Lodges: Rwindi, Mutwanga and in Goma
Campsites: Available

Garamba National Park
Although at the extreme of what may reasonably described as East Africa, Garamba is important in the region as being the last remaining location where the white rhino still occurs naturally outside southern Africa. It covers 2000 sq ml (5200 sq km) of grassland, woodland, forest and swamps. The park falls within the range of Derby's eland. Other mammals species include elephant, buffalo and kob.
Campsites: Available

1.4 Wildlife conservation in East Africa

East Africa contains one of the greatest diversities of wildlife and habitats on earth. It has a responsibility therefore not only to its own people but to the whole world to preserve this natural heritage. Conservation is fraught with contradictory issues and as soon as anyone suggests preserving something, someone else asks why. A brief examination of a few of the issues might help the visitor to Africa's parks and reserves to put into perspective some of his or her own thoughts.

Let us say right at the start that the nations of East Africa have had a good record of establishing national parks and of recognising the need to conserve wildlife. There was originally a strong degree of altruism in this but increasingly, wildlife is being looked upon as an exploitable resource. Some countries in the region have had less success than others. In spite of valiant efforts by conservation bodies in these countries, years of poaching, warfare and neglect have taken a sorry toll of animals. Uganda is a salutory lesson in this respect. Once one of the most beautiful and spectacular of safari destinations, there are now few tourists and much less for them to see in the national parks.

The questions facing conservationists in East Africa today include:
- How can we reconcile the land and food needs of a fast growing population with the desire to conserve wildlife?
- Should wildlife 'pay its way'? If so, how, and to what extent?
- Who should benefit financially from these natural resources? Government, district authorities, landholders, conservation bodies, tour operators?
- To what extent should tourism be encouraged? Are tourism and conservation in conflict or can they work together to achieve the same aims? What is the optimum level of tourism in the parks and reserves themselves? How can this be achieved or controlled in the light of national policies?
- Can or should hunting be a part of tourism and can it contribute at all to conservation?
- How can we enforce measures to improve conservation, bearing in mind the realities of human need and human greed?
- Why should we go to all this effort to please a few rich people from the developed world?

It is far from easy to offer answers to these questions but it may be useful to stimulate some thoughts in the reader's mind, knowing that there are many different points of view. In particular, the aims of conservation and tourism offer some real contradictions.

If one accepts that wildlife must earn its keep, then tourism is the first thing that comes to mind. To attract tourists from all over the world, the host country needs to be stable and to offer a reliable infrastructure such as roads, telephones, power and supplies. If the policy is to be successful, there need to be adequate facilities for accommodating visitors and for transporting them, all of which requires substantial investment. When large numbers of tourists arrive, it is also necessary to consider what effect they have on the very places they have come to see.

There are mixed feelings about the effect of large numbers of tourists on wildlife. In the peak season in Kenya's Amboseli, Mara and Samburu, as many as fifty tour buses at once may leave a lodge in search of game. If something exciting turns up, like lion or cheetah, it is encircled within moments by a crowd of buses. Current thinking suggests that such activity may not be affecting the breeding rates of the animals concerned. In the Serengeti, for instance, wild dogs utilise tour buses to conceal themselves from their prey. But have people come to experience the tranquillity of a wild place or have they come to sit in a traffic jam? Sooner or later, whatever the effect on wildlife, the tourists will go elsewhere.

It is reasonable for tourists to expect that a proportion of income to the parks and reserves be invested in improved facilities and better control of, for example, poaching. There is often little appearance of this and it is fair to question where the income goes.

Poaching, in fact, has long been the greatest obstacle to effective conservation in Africa and control of poaching ought to be a first priority. But there is ample evidence that the orgy of rhino and elephant poaching of the past decade – which still continues – has taken place under the eyes of authorities established to combat it. Naturally, governments are reluctant to admit such things but some have tried to take a stand. A fundamental issue is that of corruption. At its most simple, how can we expect someone earning the equivalent of US$150 a month to forego the chance of selling a pair of tusks at ten times this amount? The principle works at all levels.

A further dilemma facing authorities in Africa is that the per capita income of their people is very low by world standards while they have population growth rates that are among the highest in the world. If a country cannot feed its people now, what will happen in the future? It is possible that this problem is insoluble. Until very recently, the issue of birth control was perceived as a plot by the developed world to limit competitive growth. Now that people can see otherwise, it may be too late. The result for conservation will be ever increasing demands for land currently devoted to wildlife.

Land which may be uneconomic in terms of productive agriculture even now supports vast herds of wild herbivores. But local people will want that land for themselves. Elsewhere in Africa, overpopulation of both people and domestic animals has caused desertification and famine on hitherto unheard of scales. One possible solution is to utilise wild animals as a cash crop in terms of meat. This is at best a long term possibility, not only for technical and economic reasons but also because many African societies have cultural inhibitions against food from non-traditional sources.

Effective utilisation of wild meat requires either a return to a hunter-gatherer lifestyle or modern ranching methods. The former is unlikely to be politically acceptable to governments intent on pursuing national development while the latter presents a real threat to conservation. This happened in Zimbabwe, in Botswana and is beginning to be seen in Kenya. Ranchers erect long fences to demarcate their land. This has the immediate effect of stopping migrating animals literally in their tracks. These species, such as wildebeest, evolved their migratory habits to survive natural cycles of drought and plenty. Come the next drought, the wildebeest pile up against the fences and die in thousands.

Then the ranchers decide that 'vermin' like hyenas and cheetah are incompatible with meat production and they are shot out. Soon, the residual national parks are the only areas where wild animals are found – and we have already suggested that these will be eroded by people's demands for more land.

Commercial beef production is an even bigger threat. If a country wishes to export its beef, then it must not come into contact with wild animals such as buffalo or wildebeest on account of transmissible diseases such as foot and mouth. The EEC, as one major importer of beef, insists on this. Quite an irony since the EEC is a great advocate of environmental protection on its home ground. The result? Fence in the cattle, shoot out the wild animals.

In historical terms, the greatest tragedy to ungulate populations has been their eradication under tsetse fly control programmes. It now seems that tsetse flies can survive even among a dramatically depleted wild host population and they do not live only on the larger herbivores as was originally thought. In other words, large numbers of animals may have been killed for nothing.

A recent claim by animal health authorities is that trypanosomiasis, the disease carried by the flies, is the biggest single obstacle to growth in cattle and human populations. If this is so, then there can be no doubt that the tsetse fly is an irreplaceable asset in conservation terms. Vast tracts of Africa and huge numbers of animals will fall to domestic cattle if the fly is ever fully eradicated.

What of hunting? This is a topic that is guaranteed to excite tempers on all sides. It is true that some of the 'sport' hunting fraternity have engendered a poor image for their profession. Nevertheless, controlled and properly conducted safari hunting has a role in generating tourist income and in guarding an area against poaching. This is certainly the case in some countries where hunting is still allowed. There is even an argument that hunting, through limited extraction of animals, can help to increase wild populations.

More than any other part of the commercial safari world, however, hunting is difficult to control. Who can ever know if target species are being gunned down from moving vehicles instead of being carefully stalked? Who can be sure that quotas are kept? Some people may gain a certain atavistic pleasure in stalking and killing wild animals but many remain unconvinced of the positive benefits of hunting.

There may, however, be economic sense in private hunting ranches where income is generated both by allowing people to shoot animals and by selling the meat into the marketplace. This approach seems to overcome many of the objections raised against either ranching or hunting as the land will be used not for eliminating wildlife but for conserving it.

One of the most important factors in bringing about the changes in attitude and approach needed in coming generations is that of education. How will tomorrow's Africans feel to be told about the incredible wildlife they used to have? Conservation is not just for rich foreigners, it is for the children of the future. We should not deny them their heritage, even though they may choose to look at it in a different way. Perhaps this book will play its own small part in helping people to learn about and to appreciate the natural beauty of East Africa's wildlife so that they can choose to preserve it.

Many of the thoughts raised here may seem to suggest that conservation in East Africa is a lost battle. Let us look, therefore, at the present instead of the future. From the time when foreign visitors started coming to East Africa in the second half of the nineteenth century, people have been saying that the fabulous herds of wild animals were doomed. Come and see them now, they said, it can't last. But it is still fabulous. It is still awe-inspiring, breath-taking. Africa has always stretched the descriptive powers of language. To go on safari in East Africa is still one of the most memorable experiences that anyone can have. With a little bit of luck and a great deal of care, the big herds should be around for a few years yet.

1.5 Wildlife photography

There are two ways to take first class wildlife photographs. One is a matter of sheer luck. You may drive round a bend in a reserve and come upon a magnificent kudu bull. You have about half a second in which to grab the picture of a lifetime so your camera must be ready, set and poised to shoot. It is incredible how animals will simply stand and stare until you raise the camera to your eye and then bound away before you can press the button. It is often a matter of chance and good timing to find an animal well positioned, nicely lit and looking in the right direction. But it is up to you to have your camera at the ready.

The second method of getting good pictures is the one used by professionals and gives by far the best results. This is patience. Unfortunately, the casual or even keen amateur photographer does not always have enough time to wait for the right moment. To sit patiently night after night waiting for a leopard to appear at a waterhole is not a course of action open to many visitors to East Africa. But it may be the only way to get the picture. Maybe you have seen a honey badger vanish into its burrow. You sit in the vehicle, in a temperature of over 30°C, thinking of the swimming pool and cold beers back at the lodge. The badger has much more patience and will wait for you to depart before emerging.

The system of photography that is perhaps most easily used is that of opportunism, of being prepared for the unexpected. This does not guarantee pictures, but it does mean that those you take will be good or at least interesting ones. If time on a game run is limited, then the main thing is to make best use of it. When that kudu appears, you must be ready. When the safari vehicle halts right next to a herd of zebra, for instance, it is too often the case that by the time everyone has decided if they want a picture, whether the right lens is on the camera, if the film is wound on or if the lighting is right, the entire herd has turned tail and galloped into the bush in a cloud of dust. Now it is possible to get some great photographic effects with back-lit dust clouds but it is a pity how many people end up with shots of disappearing animal backsides just through being unprepared.

The secret is to be ready to shoot. When something potentially interesting turns up, shoot and ask questions later.

Equipment

A common failing is to expect too much of your equipment. This applies equally to simple 'instamatic' cameras, to high quality reflex cameras and to the best modern automatics. However sophisticated the equipment, it is the photographer behind the lens, not the electronics inside, that makes the picture.

It is quite possible to get reasonable photos with a cheap camera but they will tend to be general, scenic and people pictures. The fixed lenses of these cameras will not magnify an animal sufficiently to make a good photograph on safari. It may be possible to take shots of herds and larger mammals like elephant. A useful rule is to make the subject fill as much of the viewfinder as possible and try to keep the sun behind you. Alternatively, go for effects such as sunsets, which are often spectacular on safari. A sunset shot will come out almost whatever the lighting or exposure but do ignore any instruction the camera gives you to use a flash. These only illuminate things nearer than about ten feet or so.

Good wildlife pictures can only really be obtained with a telephoto lens of at least 200 mm. 300 mm is good but sometimes too big to hold well. Anything bigger may be difficult to handle without a great deal of care and tripods or special mounting brackets. The important thing to remember, and this applies to any camera or lens, is to keep it rock steady. The longer the lens, the more critical this is.

Exposure and film

A rule of thumb is that the shutter speed to freeze any possible camera movement should be at least the reciprocal of the focal length. In other words, a 200 mm lens will need a 200th of a second or less, a 300 mm requires a 300th, and so on. Always err on the side of fast shutter speeds. Use a 500th or a 1000th of a second and compensate by using a fast film. Remember that the available light in the tropics is much greater that in the higher latitudes. Typical lighting on safari though gives only f5.6 aperture with a shutter speed of a 500th using 64ASA film with a 300 mm lens. This is close to the baseline of what will give good pictures. A better exposure would be a 1000th of a second at f8 and this means using 400ASA film. In general, 125 or 200ASA film speeds are adequate.

This may seem quite complicated but it is important to do your figuring out beforehand. There simply isn't time when you need it. That fleeting glimpse of the leopard is much too brief for you to start working out apertures, depth of focus and camera shake.

This brings us to automatic cameras. Some people go on safari with all the latest exposure-programmed cameras, autofocus lenses and motor-drives. Sometimes they take better pictures than the folk with the instamatics. But if they do, it's not a result of the equipment. These cameras suffer just as much from camera shake and disappearing backsides. The motor-drives gobble up film that can't always be replaced, and the electronically adjusted 'ideal' exposure is a compromise that may not be right for the shot you want. Automatic cameras do have the advantage of reducing the number of variables that you need to think about as you 'grab' that leaping impala but they don't always get it right.

A bird on a branch will come out as a silhouette against the sky unless you open up the aperture by one and a half or two stops. The camera doesn't know that. In cases where the subject is swamped by the brighter light of sky or parched grass, the exposure meter is fooled. The trick is to take the reading from the darker mass of a tree or a patch of similarly lit ground. Then move the camera into position and take. Not all automatic cameras allow you to do this and some have such awkward 'back light' settings that you might as well use a manual camera.

Getting close

Converters are another thing that too many people put too much faith in. 2x and 3x multipliers are available to magnify the image in the lens. This may seem to be the answer to the problem of distant animals, small birds and so on, but it is not. Unless you can afford converters manufactured by the top lens makers themselves, and designed to accompany a specific lens, then it may not be worth bothering. Firstly, you lose two or three f.stops, which reduces your flexibility on shutter speed and increases the risk of shake. Secondly, by increasing the effective focal length, you need a shorter speed anyway to avoid blurring due to shake. Thirdly, focussing becomes more critical and finally there is nearly always a very noticeable loss of sharpness and contrast in the picture. An image on a negative can often be enlarged better into a print in an enlarger than by doubling its size in the first place by using a converter.

There is no doubt that the best wildlife pictures are obtained by getting close to the animal. This is of course open to luck and a fair amount of skill. But you can't get around the problem by using big lenses and converters unless you are an expert.

Composition

On the other hand, don't make the mistake of assuming that just because you can see an animal it will make a satisfactory picture. The eye and brain often seem to see things bigger than the film records them and too many safari photographs end up with little grey blobs that may, or may not, have been a rhino in the distance. Try to judge how large the animal appears in the viewfinder before you press the button. It can be a good idea to leave room around it for trees, habitat, scenery and so on but dots on the horizon won't be the souvenir you want when you get home.

Practical tips

If this gives the impression that wildlife photography is beyond the ability of an average photographer, then the following basic rules will help to produce acceptable results for almost everyone.

- Check and use your equipment before you go. Always try out new equipment while you have access to the shop you bought it from. Always carry spare batteries for your camera – they all seem to need them these days.
- Take more film than you expect to use. An excited 'first-timer' on safari may easily use up a film per day and it is not always obtainable where you are going. A keen amateur can expect to use up to ten rolls of film on a two week safari.
- If you plan to use a zoom or telephoto lens bigger than 300 mm, take a tripod or beanbag to rest on. The beanbag can be placed on the car windowsill or edge of the game-viewing hatch, and provides a solid rest for a long lens, providing the engine of the vehicle is not running.
- Never let the camera rest in the sun. The heat builds up quickly and melts the film emulsion, ruining both picture and camera. Change film in the shade.
- Wrap your camera in a towel to protect it against jolts and use a plastic bag to keep out dust when it's not in use. A camera case does not give enough protection against safari conditions.
- Store equipment in a soft bag rather than a hard aluminium case. Bouncing around on dirt roads soon shows where the hard edges and sharp corners are.
- Once on safari, travel with your camera ready. This means putting on the right lens that you expect to need, taking a typical aperture reading to go with your chosen shutter speed, or setting to auto. Take off the lens cap and wind on the film. Unless you are driving, keep your camera on your knee ready to use.

- Do make sure that the film is engaged properly on the sprockets. In the excitement of changing film during a lion kill, it is only too easy to do it wrongly. A quick check is to watch the rewind knob while you wind on the film. This should rotate as you wind on once the slack has been taken up.
- If you have plenty of film, a good rule is to snap quickly any animal that looks interesting, then compose a more careful second shot if the creature is obliging enough to stay put. The worst that can happen this way is that you take more pictures than you really need but then again you just might catch that ace shot that everyone else misses.
- When you have time to be careful, look at the horizon in the viewfinder to make sure that it is horizontal. It can also appear to cut an animal in half, with bland grass in the lower half of the shot and blank sky in the top half. It can be better to try to eliminate the sky completely, or get the horizon line either one third or two thirds into the frame.
- Focus on the eye of an animal. This is the part that everyone will notice in the final result. If possible, wait until there is a bright catchlight in the eye. This makes the photo come alive.
- Try to catch animals in poses that are not static but show something of their behaviour. This is far from easy, but a zebra kicking its legs is ten times more interesting than a side-on shot doing nothing.
- When hand-holding a zoom or telephoto, always support the barrel of the lens as if it were a rifle. Keep your elbows tucked in and breathe steadily, holding your breath as you shoot. This way, you will go as far as you can to avoid camera shake and a blurred image.
- However good your camera, the picture will be improved if the scene is well lit. This usually means having the sun shining from behind you to light whatever you are looking at. But in spite of what some people say, it is possible to get good shots even when the sun is overhead at midday.
- Bring along a 'puffer' brush to clean dust from the lens regularly. Don't use fingers or handkerchiefs.

Finally, remember that with good lighting, careful composition, familiarity with your camera and a little bit of luck, even that 'buck' shot could be a winner.

Minimum shutter speeds to avoid camera shake

Focal length of lens, mm	Minimum shutter speed, secs.
50	1/ 60
100	1/125
200	1/250
300	1/500
400	1/500
500	1/500

In the following pages there is a section of black and white and colour photographs taken on safari by the author.

The African plains buffalo presents a formidable sight at close range. (page 78)

The forest buffalo of central and west Africa is smaller and has much shorter horns than its East African cousin. (page 78)

A magnificent greater kudu feeding in Lake Bogoria National Reserve. (page 80)
A young male sitatunga. The horns will twist further and grow longer as the animal ages. (page 84)

A female sable antelope with young in Shimba Hills. (page 87)

A handsomely marked beisa oryx. The fringe eared oryx differs only in having a black tuft at the end of each ear. (page 88)

Beisa oryx rest in the shade of an acacia tree in Samburu National Reserve. (page 88)
The 'migration' in the Masai Mara. Numbers and movements of wildebeest vary from season to season but the herds usually reach the Mara between August and October. (page 89)

The Mara River takes it toll of the migrating herds.

A well-worn male kongoni in Nairobi National Park. These hartebeest do not often permit such a close approach. (page 90)

A male waterbuck. It could be defassa or common from this angle but is in fact defassa at Lake Nakuru. (page 94)

Male bohor reedbuck in the Serengeti. (page 98)

A male sable antelope indulging in 'flehmen', or lip-baring, as a prelude to mating. Shimba Hills National Reserve, Kenya. (page 87)

A male red lechwe fleeing across floodplains in southern Zambia. (page 95)

Young impala. Amboseli National Park, Kenya. (page 101)

A female gerenuk hides in thornbush near the Tana River. Meru National Park, Kenya. (page 102)

An adult male Grant's gazelle with particularly fine horns. In parts of the region, these animals' horns may be almost parallel or widely diverging. Masai Mara National Reserve, Kenya. (page 103)

A common duiker. These retiring and often nocturnal antelope are quite common in some localities but frequently inhabit dense bush. (page 113)

Reticulated giraffe posed obligingly in front of the distant glaciers on Mt Kenya. Samburu/Buffalo Springs National Reserve, Kenya. (page 126)

A small herd of Grevy's zebra plodding home for the night. Samburu/Buffalo Springs National Reserve, Kenya. (page 128)

A mother black rhino and her offspring in Ngorongoro crater. The crater wall forms an impressive photographic backdrop. (page 131)

One of the classic sights of East Africa. Red-dusted elephants coming to drink at the Kilaguni waterhole in Tsavo West. (page 133)

Elephant poaching continues at an alarming rate throughout the region. This picture was taken in the heart of Amboseli National Park in 1980. The vultures don't know how to penetrate the thick hide. (page 133)

A female cheetah with a restless youngster. Note the raised hackles on the kitten. These persist until the animal is quite well grown. Masai Mara National Reserve, Kenya. (page 144)

A silverback mountain gorilla peeks at intruders over the dense jungle vegetation. Volcanoes National Park, Rwanda. (page 164)

A troup of black and white colobus showing their distinctive white mantle and tails. Arusha National Park, Tanzania. (page 172)

The forested lower slopes of Mt Meru provide a habitat for Masai giraffe. Arusha National Park, Tanzania.

The author on safari by the Uaso Ngiro River. This northern part of Kenya provides some wild, spectacular and rarely visited scenery. Shaba National Reserve, Kenya.

A male gerenuk in Samburu. This species is common throughout northern Kenya. (page 102)
A group of male Grant's gazelle in Masai Mara. (page 103)

A male Thomson's gazelle. Note the black stripe and the black tail. (page 104)
An alert steenbok in the instant before flight. (page 107)

A close-up of a warthog's face reveals the twin tusks used for rooting tubers from the ground. (page 122)

One of these hippos stood on the crocodile's tail and was seen off with a sharp snap. (page 124)

Grevy's zebra in Samburu. These are an endangered species. (page 128)
A black rhino with an unusually long second horn. The raised tail could indicate an imminent charge. (page 131)

A year old elephant feeds from its mother's mammary glands which are located between the forelegs. (page 133)

A young spotted hyena suns itself at the entrance to its burrow. (page 134)

A striped hyena captured with a standard lens and a flashgun and a certain amount of luck in focussing. (page 135)

Black backed jackal. Sometimes called silver backed because in older specimens, the hair on the back shows grey. (page 138)

A bat eared fox is interrupted in its hunting but is unconcerned about the herd of tsessebe in the background. (page 141)

Two faces of Africa — the wild and the urban — seen from Nairobi National Park.

A serval hunting frogs in a swampy area of Ngorongoro crater. (page 145)
A civet with a raised dorsal crest. Standard lens and flash. (page 149)

A large spotted genet caught by flash from the doorway of my tent. (page 151)
Mountain gorilla suckling young in Rwanda's Volcanoes National Park. (page 164)

Rock hyrax at Hell's Gate National Park where these animals are particularly approachable. (page 186)

A ground squirrel uses its bushy tail as a parasol as it feeds in the heat of the day. (page 182)

1.6 Watching wildlife

There are some myths about watching wildlife and there are some guidelines which can help everyone find and enjoy the many species of animals which East Africa's parks and reserves are renowned for.

First, the myths about early rising and staying in camp at midday. You don't have to get up at dawn to see animals. This may be a good time to see nocturnal species before they retire for the day and lion often hunt soon after sunrise but African dawns can be cold, grey and unexciting. Admittedly, breakfast does taste better after an early game run.

You CAN see things and even photograph them in the middle of the day. The light may be nearly vertical but that doesn't always matter. It may be hot. Some animals are less active at this time. But the great thing is that few other people will be about. You can watch cheetah hunt in the very hottest hours while everyone else is having lunch and elephants often bathe while other people are taking a siesta. However, the best times tend to be in the golden light of a late afternoon.

Tour or do it yourself

One question that many people ask themselves is whether to go on safari with a commercial operator or to do it themselves. There are advantages in both approaches. A professional guide should be able to locate animals and drive the safari vehicle to allow you to take the photographs you want. You may not have to do your own cooking. But all of this depends on the calibre of the company you are with and the driver you get. Try therefore to speak to people who have been on safari. Word of mouth is a powerful recommendation.

Doing it yourself has some immediate drawbacks. What sort of vehicle, where can you hire it from, where do you stay, where and what do you eat, how do you know where to go, how do you find the animals? But there is one enormous advantage. You can go where you like and spend as long as you wish. The thrill of finding animals yourself is hard to beat.

There are some excellent safari operators who will provide even this level of personal service although it can be costly.

Lodges or camping

Another choice concerns accommodation. There are three basic options and the decision is a matter of personal preference. The luxury lodges that exist in some parts of East Africa are an experience in themselves. In other places, the luxury is not even skin deep. Without doubt, the Kenyan game lodges offer the highest standards but they are getting very crowded at most times of the year. Some of them bait animals in order to guarantee that visitors will see certain unusual species. One lodge even has a timetable. Genet 6.30, white tailed mongoose 8.00, leopard 11.30. The choice is yours.

Some countries have self-catering cottages or bungalows available for safari visitors. These offer a useful compromise. Those in the Malaŵi parks are particularly good, offering clean and adequate accommodation with the services of a cook thrown in. The Kenyan 'bandas' are rather more basic and it is necessary to be fully self-contained, even to the extent of bringing your own water in some places. They do however give the opportunity to keep all your belongings locked up away from monkeys and predatory humans.

Camping under canvas is, according to many people, the only way to experience Africa. You can camp alone or with a safari company and it is nowhere near as dangerous or uncomfortable as some may think. It is necessary to be well equipped, however, and this influences the type of vehicle you use. It is sad that the pleasure of being in the great African outdoors is nowadays compromised by risks not from wild animals but from people. Some cheaper safari operators are monopolising and littering campsites to the extent that park authorities are beginning to think twice about the value of such facilities.

Unguarded tents are liable to be ransacked in many parts of East Africa. Even if the local populace is friendly, baboons and vervet monkeys quickly become tame and aggressive, especially if foodstuffs are left in camp.

Personally, I find the excitement of camping, especially at night, to be unmatched. We've had lions in camp, herds of wildebeest cantering through, hyenas snuffling at our feet – and still I go back for more. The drawback is that security is beginning to be a real problem.

Vehicles

If you do choose to go on safari yourself, don't be too concerned about the type of vehicle you use. You don't need a Land Rover to visit many of the parks and reserves. A reliable saloon car may be quite adequate. Four-wheel drive is only really necessary if you are travelling in the rainy season or planning to go well off the beaten track. If you have a larger party, the minibuses used by some of the commercial operators are amazing and will go most places that a four-wheel drive would go. My own preference is for a Land Rover but then we do go off the beaten track and have learnt over the years how to carry out whatever repairs may be necessary.

Seasons

The best times for game-viewing are without doubt in the dry seasons. This is because animals tend to concentrate near available water or grazing. Also, although it may be hot, it is usually more pleasant when it is not raining.

On the other hand, these times can be very dusty and are often the most popular with other visitors. Rainy seasons do not always mean days and days of grey skies and muddy roads. There can be some very pleasant periods and a surprising amount of animals may be encountered. There are fewer people and prices are usually much cheaper.

Traditionally, July and August and the Christmas period have been popular times for visitors from Europe and north America but this is changing. People come at all times of the year now. Nevertheless, if exciting game-viewing is your priority, study the rainfall periods and arrange your safari towards the end of a dry season.

The seasons are not always reliably predictable and there can be great variation even within a country but, in general, dry seasons are as follows:

Kenya, Tanzania and Uganda	June-October and January-March
Malaŵi and Zambia	May-October
Rwanda and Zaïre	Rains most of the time but may be drier January-March and June-September

Finding animals

Most people find that simply driving slowly around the parks and reserves produces sufficient interest, almost by chance. But there are a few tips that can help to increase your success rate. Riverbanks and waterholes attract animals

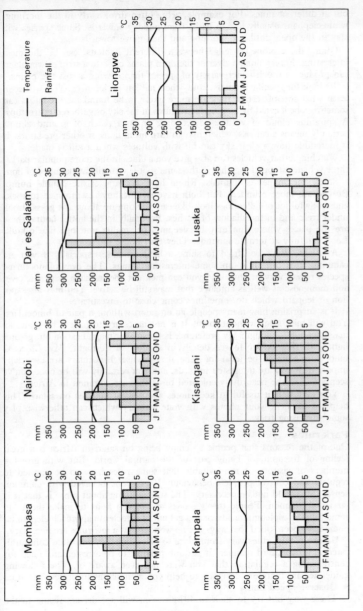

but at different times. For example, zebra often drink early in the morning, while elephant usually like to bathe from midday onwards. Some species will stay in the open until late morning and then move towards shade.

Often, the ecotone, or edge between different habitats, can be the most interesting. Forest along a river or the open plains close to a strip of woodland can produce a much wider variety of species than driving across the plains.

To look for specific animals, study their habitat preferences. You will soon learn what sort of terrain they are more likely to be found in. Predators can sometimes be located by looking for vultures in the sky or gathered in treetops. A spiralling cloud of vultures descending on to a patch of ground almost certainly means a carcass, which may in turn mean lions or other predators. It is incredible how a clear sky can fill with vultures when a kill is made.

Watching other vehicles can also give you a clue. In the more popular parks, three vehicles stopped together in the same spot is virtually a guarantee of lion.

Study the shapes of animals. Rhino have a characteristic double hump. Buffalo are more rounded. But both have an uncanny resemblance to rocks and an awful lot of fallen logs look like ears sticking up above the grass. Look under trees and in the shadow of bushes. Especially in the hotter hours, these are the places where lion may be sleeping, or smaller antelope like dikdik. Look carefully at termite mounds. They may house mongooses.

At night, don't be afraid to shine a light around. Especially if you are camping, this can show up some interesting things. The eyes of nocturnal species reflect very brightly and you can pick out species such as genet, civet and mongoose as well as antelope that may still be active. You may also spot lion or leopard which do sometimes come close to investigate.

It is surprising how many people go on safari without a pair of binoculars. You will miss a lot without them. It is not necessary to have a big pair. 8x magnification is enough. My preference is for smaller magnification but greater light gathering power to see details in shadow or at night. My 7.5 x 42 binoculars seem to be ideal for general safari use. Binoculars are especially important if you are interested in birds, and you certainly will be once you've seen a few of the beautifully coloured birds that are common in Africa.

You may find it useful to keep notes about what you see on safari. This helps to reconcile your photos with your memory which can otherwise play some surprising tricks.

Park rules

One of the reasons that people so enjoy being on safari in Africa is a great feeling of freedom, of being part of the natural world. But with growing numbers of visitors, it is inevitable that some rules have to be applied to regulate and control people's behaviour. If everyone behaved with common sense, this would not be necessary. The strange thing about sense is that it is far from common. People throw stones at sleeping lions to make them 'do something'. People ignore advice and get out of vehicles to approach elephants. Some have been killed that way. It's no wonder that a few rules are necessary.

Unfortunately, rules vary from place to place and they are often communicated in a haphazard manner. It is quite possible to be arrested and fined for contravening a regulation that you were not even aware of. The following guidelines are therefore designed to help you as much as to protect wildlife.

- **Observe speed limits**

    These vary but try to stick to 40 kph. You will see drivers racing to the lodges much faster than this. They shouldn't. It causes corrugations on the roads, generates plumes of dust, stops them seeing things and can be dangerous to the occupants, to animals and to other vehicles.

- **Keep to marked roads**

Unless you know that driving off-road is allowed, which it is in some places. The reason for this is that vegetation may be damaged in some areas by the pressure of tyres. In Amboseli, for example, a single set of tyre tracks can be seen years later. It may also be difficult driving off-road. If you get stuck, think about all the dangers and inconvenience trying to get help.

- **Remember the animals are wild**

Do not approach them on foot, even as an experiment. Elephant, rhino and lion will simply charge you and that will be that. If animals approach you, in camp for example, it is a different matter. So long as they are aware of your presence, it is very unlikely they will do any damage. The real danger is if you come between a mother and its young. Protective action may require removing you from the scene.

- **Do not feed animals or leave food in tents**

Even if you want to get a nice picture of a baboon, do not be tempted to offer it food. You are simply signing its death warrant. Monkeys, and even elephants, become accustomed to the presence of tourists and may associate them with food. The animals may then start to raid camps and lodges, inevitably causing damage, and eventually have to be removed.

I once watched a party of tourists having lunch at a lodge in Kenya. Prominent signs all around the room said *DO NOT FEED THE BABOONS* in several languages. In spite of this, someone held out a bread roll for a baboon which was waiting outside the protective wall. Immediately, the baboon leapt on to the wall and from there on to the table, scattering glasses, plates and tourists. Some people laughed, others screamed. But the baboon would get the blame.

- **Do not leave litter**

This should be obvious. A national park is intended to be free from all human influences. It rarely is, but litter is under your control. Take it away.

- **Do not drive at night**

Never drive after dark, unless it is specifically permitted. It is dangerous on account of poor roads and animals that you may not see. It is surprising just how many vehicles one sees driving at night in some national parks. Many of these may be park staff but even they shouldn't be doing it unless there is very good reason.

- **Don't encourage your driver to break the rules**

Your driver wants to please you and may be tempted to break the rules, especially if you reward him. But remember, you can be fined and thrown out of the park. He can lose his job.

- **Consider other people and why they have come**

If everyone did this, there would be no need for rules. People come to experience nature, not other tourists. You don't want them to disturb you, so please avoid disturbing others. Don't make noises, don't scare the animals, be patient and take your turn if it's crowded.

- **Please do not buy ivory or other wildlife products. It is only because people do that there are so few elephants left**

These rules are largely a matter of common sense and if everyone follows them, we can all enjoy watching the wonderful wildlife we have come to see.

1.7 Close encounters in the bush

So many crazy but wonderful things happen on safari that it's no wonder people are either enthralled or bemused by the stories they hear. People who spend a lot of their time in the bush get a reputation for being a little crazy themselves. Even so, half of the fun of a safari is sharing stories around the campfire — and adding to the fund of tales for next time. These are a few highlights from some of my own safaris to give a flavour of this 'other world' that so many enjoy once they've had a taste of it. Incidentally, these anecdotes are all true. There's not even any exaggeration.

We usually go to bed quite early on safari, to be able to rise with the sun. One night, I was soundly asleep when I was woken by a tremendous crash of glass and metal. Hastily looking out through the mosquito net door of the tent, I shone a light towards the source of the noise and saw something I could barely believe. One of our group had left a fridge outside, to give more space in the vehicle where he was sleeping. The fridge was full of meat and other perishables but was securely locked and had been liberally sprayed with insecticide to disguise the odour of food. It was connected to a heavy gas cylinder. In spite of all these precautions, a spotted hyena had grasped the fridge in its jaws and was trying to carry it away. The crash that had woken me, and by now everyone else, was a lamp attached to the gas cylinder falling as the hyena dragged the whole lot behind it.

The power of a hyena's jaws is one of legends of the bush and this feat certainly proved it. The loaded fridge was too heavy for one person to lift on his own but the hyena had it in its mouth. I leapt out of bed and chased the animal off with a wooden mallet. It loped reluctantly into the bushes but as I shone the lamp around, there seemed to be dozens of pairs of eyes reflecting back at us. Clearly the hyenas had learnt that campers spelled food and this was a good reminder to us never to leave any foodstuffs out, or inside the tents.

After the excitement had died down, the fridge had been restored to its usual position inside the Land Rover, and everyone had gone back to bed, I lay awake, watching through the netting. Hyenas may seem cowardly, but they usually come back when the coast is clear. Silently, the huge beast returned. At least it looked huge from my prone position on the ground. It padded around the tents, carefully stepping over guy ropes, sniffed at the campfire and trotted towards me. The hyena came to within a few feet of my mosquito net until it seemed that he and I were almost nose to nose. My heart was pounding and I hardly dared to breathe. I sat frozen, the mallet in one hand and the torch in the other, waiting. I have no doubt that if I had moved, the hyena would have fled, but with all wild animals, discretion is very much the better part of survival. At last, the beast turned away, carefully picked up a shoe that someone had left out and trotted away with it in its mouth, for all the world like an overgrown puppy.

We found the shoe, undamaged, the next morning. Hyena spoor was all over the place but most people were blissfully unaware that these animals had passed within inches of where they slept, separated only by a thin sheet of canvas. This proved to me that even a large carnivore will not normally attack people in their tents. Unless they leave them open, of course. The fridge bears the deep indentations of the hyena's fangs to this day.

On the same safari, I think it was the very next evening, an elephant wandered into camp while we were chatting around the fire. Everyone looked up, rather alarmed, wondering what to do — and, more importantly, what the elephant would do. We sat still and watched. The first move the elephant made was to feel all over the surface of a table with the tip of its trunk. Maybe there were a few crumbs. One lady had left her sunglasses on the table and was by now somewhat concerned. The elephant carefully picked these up, tasted them, smelled them, peered at them and then replaced them on the table quite undamaged.

The gas lamp that had been smashed by the hyena on the previous night had been repaired but now the elephant decided to take a look at it. It had been put on top of the Land Rover out of reach of hyenas but the elephant had no trouble locating it. Crash went the new glass. Enough was enough. We were running out of lamp glasses. I picked up a flaming bough from the fire, walked towards the elephant with this smoking in front of me and held it towards the elephant's trunk. It smelled the smoke and quite calmly turned and walked slowly away. I was very relieved that it had not become alarmed and rampaged through our tents and vehicles. Like the hyena, it was obviously accustomed to people — and food.

Suddenly there was a muffled yell from behind a bush. One of the party had been quietly 'communing with nature' when he looked up to see the huge grey creature bearing down on him. The elephant passed without a pause but our friend's constipation was cured at a stroke.

Campsites in some reserves are fenced and controlled but camping out in the true wilderness can be the greatest adventure and not dangerous so long as one respects the wild animals. This was brought home to me on another occasion when it had been raining fairly heavily for several hours. We had struggled to keep the fire alight and now that darkness had fallen, we stood a little miserably around the flames trying to dry off and keep warm. Now, many animals, especially cats, don't much like wet grass and they tend to come out on to the roads after rain. Suddenly we heard a lion roar not far away. It was answered by that evocative gruff call that descends in a series of grunts and brings goose-pimples to the skin. The lion were near and coming closer.

People have trouble in such circumstances believing that when you can hear lion like this, it means they are not actively hunting. They keep quiet when it matters. Well we kept pretty quiet too at this juncture. Two or three of the group vanished into one of the Land Rovers but the rest of us stayed by the fire. The sounds of the lions came closer and closer. Their calls can carry for miles but it was as if we could hear every whisker on their faces, they were so close. The people in the vehicle shone a light out across the track and called to us. We looked up in time to see four lions skulking past our camp barely twenty feet from where we stood. They were highly nervous and, disturbed by the light, ran off into the wet bush. Hardly the display of courage you would expect from the so-called king of the jungle.

Camping sites can be quite eventful especially if they are near water. One place we sometimes camp is right on the banks of a river and hippo can often be heard there, snorting away in the water. One night, again while we were chatting around the fire, there was a curious whirring sound and a heavy pungent aroma floated in the cool air. I took a light and went to investigate.

The track that passed the camp was narrow, barely wide enough for a vehicle. I shone the lamp along it. A pair of orange eyes glowed in the dark but it took several seconds to realise that a vast bulk lay behind them. It was a hippo and it completely filled the track.

With a degree of manoeuvring that made a three-point turn seem simple, the hippo spun around and plodded away. Bits of scattered straw showed the source of the odour. When hippo defecate, they flick their tails rapidly from side to side to break up the dung. This was the whirring sound we had heard. The smell was powerful and hung in the air for hours.

It is often thought that a campfire will help to keep animals away but the opposite is more often the case. This hippo and the wet lions may well have been attracted out of curiosity to the light of the fire. I have seen a baboon thrust its hand right into a blazing fire to retrieve a foil-wrapped potato. Genets and mongooses regularly snuffle round our fires to see what scraps there may be.

Snakes are another source of safari mythology. We have hardly ever seen snakes on safari. Three or four times, maybe. Certainly they are much less alarming to see than to think about. On one trip, some of our group were sunning themselves on a pole bridge across a narrow stream. It was a pleasant spot and if they were too hot, they could roll into the cool water, which we knew was free of bilharzia, even if there were hippos there. Somebody eased himself into a more comfortable position and, moving his mattress, felt something that was neither bridge nor foam rubber. It was a cobra. Luckily, the snake was as lethargic as the people and reluctantly slithered under the poles. A few people changed their minds about sunbathing but it was the last we saw of the snake.

We nearly ran over a python once. The wheel just caught its tail but pressed it into the sand and caused no harm. The python had only recently shed its skin and was a beautiful mottled colour. It too seemed sleepy and we were able to take a close look, knowing that pythons are not poisonous. At six feet long it was impressive but nowhere near fully grown.

It is not always the animals that threaten danger. The sausage tree, *Kigelia africana*, grows in moist locations throughout much of eastern and southern Africa. It is a lovely tree, green and shady in the dry season when other trees are bare. We had not noticed, however, how local Africans avoid it. The fruit of this tree, which give rise to its common name, resemble huge sausages. They are up to two feet long and weigh several kilos. On this particular safari, we had with us an adventurous and fit gentleman who was no less than 70 years old. He had gone to great lengths to persuade us that he was a suitable candidate for a safari into remote parts of Africa and so far he had done as well as anyone. One lunchtime, we stopped for a picnic and without thinking, set everything up in the shade of a sausage tree. After lunch, everyone felt like a snooze, it was so hot.

Our 70-year-old was fast asleep when, with a whoosh like an artillery shell, a well-grown sausage detached itself from the tree, fell and struck him on the chest. A few inches higher or lower and the sausage could have killed him. But ribs are designed to protect one's insides and that is what they did. We were two days' travel from any kind of medical assistance but our friend was not to be put off by a bit of pain. We strapped him up, fed him paracetamol and he travelled the rest of the safari with barely a moan, insisting that we did not send him home early.

It was more than a week later that he was able to see a doctor who confirmed what we all suspected. The sausage had broken two ribs.

'Never in all my life,' said the doctor, 'has anyone come to me complaining of being attacked by a sausage.'

It is the unexpected encounters with animals that provide the poignant memories, never more so than when one forsakes the confines of a vehicle and takes to one's own feet. This is no doubt why, in some parts of Africa, walking safaris are growing in popularity. From one such safari came one of my own most lasting memories, being touched by a mountain gorilla who wanted to know what I was made of.

Often, a feeling of sheer terror is what makes a safari such a different experience from the usual routine of urban life. We were once camped not far from a waterhole. There did not seem to be much game around and, after dark, four of us wandered over to the waterhole and climbed a termite mound with the intention of watching for a while to see if any nocturnal species would turn up. It was a classically beautiful African night with a full moon bathing the scene in an unearthly glow. A big fig tree grew out of the termite mound, or more probably, the termites had built up against the tree. Clumps of other lovely trees stood around the water. Insects were buzzing softly but there were no biting mosquitoes. Even without any animals, it was a wonderful, peaceful place.

The elephants came so silently that they were in the water before we knew it. There were about thirty of them, a breeding herd with females and a whole range of youngsters from tiny babies to frisky teenagers. They drank and bathed right in front of us, quite oblivious to our presence on the termite hill. The elephants were so close it felt as if we could have reached out and touched them. We trembled in silence. In the eerie moonlight, it was an unreal scene, like watching a film. No one dared even to breathe.

We tried, ever so quietly, to edge further up into the fig tree. We were already higher than the elephant but they could easily have reached us if they had wanted to. We made not a sound. Suddenly, the middle-aged cow elephant that was in charge of the herd glanced towards us. There was a slight crosswind so she could not catch our scent but, although elephants do not have great eyesight, it was clear she could see something. She took a few steps towards us. And still we made no sound.

The elephant made no movement nor sound herself. She just stood, trying to make us out. Abruptly, the rest of the herd ceased its splashing and bathing and silently filed out the way they had come. The matriarch turned and followed them. There was absolutely nothing to obstruct our view. We could clearly see that there had been no movement, no sound, no signal of any sort to tell the herd to go.

It has sometimes been suggested that elephants possess telepathic or other abilities that we cannot begin to guess at. After this, I can well believe it. We have a great deal to learn from our wild friends.

1.8 Some fascinating facts and further reading

The fastest mammal

The cheetah is accepted as the fastest mammal, not only in Africa but worldwide. It has been suggested that the cheetah can achieve speeds of 100 kph (60 mph) but this is unlikely as measured speeds are in the region of 70 kph (45 mph). This can be sustained only for a few seconds. The cheetah needs such speed to run down its prey which it normally hunts in broad daylight and in open plains. Cheetah first stalk carefully to within a hundred metres or so and burst into action for the remaining distance. If, as often happens, the prey escapes, by leaping or scattering into bushes, then the cheetah is faced with another long stalk.

Other predators such as lion, hyena and wild dog can reach about 40–50 kph (25–30 mph) and many antelope can do better than this. Elephant and rhino can certainly charge at this sort of speed.

The fastest antelope is the tsessebe. I have watched tsessebe galloping like racehorses but was unable to clock their speed. It was probably about 60–70 kph (40–45 mph).

The biggest mammal

The African elephant is the largest land mammal in the world (some whales are much bigger). The largest recorded measured 13' (3.96 m) at the shoulder and had an astonishing mass of 12 tonnes. A more typical maximum is around 6 – 7 tonnes. To gain this enormous bulk, elephant need to spend up to 18 hours a day feeding. They may consume 250 kg (550 lb) of vegetable matter per day and 150 litres of water. A 10-year-old female has been recorded as depositing over 100 kg (220 lb) of dung in a 24 hour period.

Baby elephants weigh in at around 120 kg (265 lb). Armand Denis in his autobiography claimed he was one of the few people to have carried an elephant when he manhandled an orphaned baby into the back of his car.

The longest tusk ever measured from an elephant was 11'6" (3.5 m) along the curve and the heaviest pair weighed 102 kg (225 lb) and 109 kg (240 lb). These came from Kenya. Tusks like these are very rarely seen nowadays.

The tallest mammal is the giraffe with a record height of 20' (6.1 m).

The longest lived mammal

The elephant again takes honours here, living up to, and sometimes beyond, 60 years. Rhino may live 40 years, hippo and zebra 30, giraffe 25, hyenas 20, apes and monkeys 20, warthog 15 and antelope typically 8 – 12.

The most widespread mammals

Of all the mammals covered in this book, only four occur throughout the entire East African region. These are leopard, genet, slender mongoose and porcupine. This does not mean that these species can be found everywhere, as they have certain habitat preferences, but they are the most adaptable in terms of the variety of habitats they can exploit.

The buffalo, bushbuck, bushpig, hippo, elephant and civet are also widespread but again are restricted to specific habitats which means that their distribution is discontinuous. This applies especially to hippo and elephant which are largely incompatible with human settlement. Those species which are solitary, nocturnal and confined to forests seem to do best — in other words their habits are completely unlike humans'. Even these species will decline as forests are felled.

The rarest mammals

Some small mammals such as Meller's mongoose, bushy tailed mongoose and the striped weasel appear to be very rare as they are known only from relatively few specimens. This does not necessarily mean that they are, in fact, rare. It is possible that they have habits that make them difficult to find and perhaps they are confined to areas or habitats that are restricted in size and accessibility.

On this basis, duiker species such as Abbot's and Zanzibar are also rare as they are confined to very small, densely forested areas.

Just because a species is rarely seen, it does not follow that it is rare. For example, not many people commonly see leopard on safari, except in one or two favoured locations, yet this is one of the most widespread of animals and has been removed from the endangered list.

Endangered species in the region include the Tana River sub-species of mangabey and red colobus, gorilla, chimpanzee, hirola, lechwe, tsessebe, roan, cheetah, wild dog, Grevy's zebra, Derby's eland and both rhinos. Most of these have small populations restricted to threatened locations. Some, such as the chimpanzee, gorilla, cheetah and rhinos have also suffered severely from hunting and poaching. It's a depressingly long list.

The black rhino takes the record for the most dramatic decline in numbers. Watched by the world's conservation authorities, poaching reduced its numbers by perhaps 80 — 90% during the late seventies and early eighties. The white rhino, which occurred within the region in Uganda, southern Sudan and north eastern Zaïre, is now thought only to occur in Garamba National Park in Zaïre. Even a small introduced herd in Meru National Park in Kenya has been depleted by poachers in spite of being guarded.

The lesson to be learned is one of complacency: the elephant, currently considered numerous, is under severe pressure throughout its range and could easily go the same way in the near future.

The most numerous mammals

It is difficult to be certain which species takes this honour. There are several contenders. Anyone watching the wildebeest migration in Serengeti would have little doubt that this animal is the most numerous. Figures are quoted in the region of two million for the number of wildebeest in this area. But this is no more than an estimate. Even the big migrating herds are rarely larger than several tens of thousands and wildebeest do not occur in the same concentrations in most other parts of the region.

Lechwe occur in herds of ten thousand or so in parts of Zambia but are very restricted in locality. Impala are without doubt the most widespread of the herd species and, throughout the region, certainly amount to large numbers. Thomson's gazelle migrate with the wildebeest and can number tens of thousands but again they are restricted in distribution. Buffalo occur in large herds and are widely spread. They are probably a serious contender in the population stakes.

The most dangerous mammal

This has long been a subject of debate, especially around hunters' campfires. The dubious honour for the most dangerous animal is often shared between the lion and the buffalo. Buffalo, especially if wounded or injured, can be very cunning and seem to be able to deliberately circle and attack anyone following them. However, in practice, lion are only dangerous if stumbled on in the bush and uninjured buffalo tend to flee rather than attack. But it is dangerous to generalise and all wild animals must be treated with great respect.

So far as Africa's indigenous human population is concerned, hippo and crocodile between them account for more fatalities than all other wildlife put together. These are only normally encountered near water. On safari, only lions or elephant present any real risk. Fatalities from either are rare.

The elephant takes the place as the most potentially dangerous mainly on account of its size. It is the only animal capable of turning over a vehicle and although usually fairly placid, certain individuals can be temperamental and unpredictable. If an elephant decides to attack someone on foot, there is little hope of escape. This is why it is important never to approach elephant on foot, especially if there are young about.

Bibliography

These are the books I have consulted in order to add to my own observations in compiling this book. Some are out of date and some are incomplete but they all contain useful information. I have taken the accumulated information on distribution from these and other sources as the basis for my own maps.

A Field Guide to the National Parks of East Africa, J G Williams, Collins, 1981.

A Field Guide to the Mammals of Africa and Madagascar, T Haltenorth and H Diller, Collins, 1972.

A Field Guide to the Larger Mammals of Africa, J Dorst and P Dandelot, Collins, 1980.

The Mammals of Rhodesia, Zambia and Malaŵi, R H N Smithers, Collins, 1966.

Land Mammals of Southern Africa – A Field Guide, R H N Smithers, Macmillan 1986.

The Mammals of the Southern African Subregion, R H N Smithers, University of Pretoria, 1983.

Signs of the Wild, C Walker, C Struik, 1981.

Animals of East Africa, C T Astley Maberly, Hodder and Stoughton, 1971.

The Wildlife Parks of Africa, N Luard, Michael Joseph, 1985.

East African Mammals, Vols 1, 11A, 11B, 111A, 111B and 111C, J Kingdon, Academic Press, 1971–1982.

Africa, A Natural History, L Brown, Hamish Hamilton, 1965.

Selected related titles from Macmillan

Macmillan also publish the following maps and guides covering East and Central Africa:

Maps:

Kenya Tourist Map	(ISBN 0-333-39359-7)
Amboseli National Park Map	(ISBN 0-333-44498-1)
Masai Mara National Reserve Map	(ISBN 0-333-44500-7)
Tsavo East and West National Parks Map	(ISBN 0-333-44499-X)
Wallmap of East Africa	(ISBN 0-333-33361-6)
Tanzania Tourist Map	(Forthcoming)

Guides:

The Nairobi Guide K. Macintyre	(ISBN 0-333-41987-1)
Malaŵi Wildlife, Parks and Reserves Judy Carter	(ISBN 0-333-43349-1)

1.9 Classification of mammals

The members of the animal kingdom have been classified by scientists into a number of categories and it can be of interest even to a layman to observe differences and similarities between species and to speculate on the reasons for them. Amongst other things, the study of relationships can throw light on evolutionary traits and show how environmental factors can influence not only behaviour but also appearance.

The hierarchy of classification categories within the animal kingdom is:

Order
Family
Sub-family
Tribe
Genus
Species
Sub-species or race

The notes on classification given here relate only to mammal species from East Africa. Each category may contain members from elsewhere in Africa or the world. Mammals are animals which suckle their young on milk from the mother's mammary glands. They are typically warm blooded, air breathing vertebrates. All living African mammals are placental and nurture the embryo from a placenta. (See the chart on pages 66–67.)

Order EVEN TOED UNGULATES *Artiodactyla*

The even toed ungulates form the largest mammal order covered in this book and members of it are among the most numerous that are commonly seen. The common characteristics of this diverse range of animals are that they carry their weight mainly on two of four toes and they are all herbivores. The two toes show in the spoor as a split or cloven hoof. Hippo, also placed in this order, show all four toes in their spoor.

Most of these species are ruminants, or animals which 'chew the cud'. These species typically possess a four chambered stomach which digests their food in separate stages, with secondary chewing carried out to aid re-digestion. This process allows them to extract maximum nutrition from otherwise difficult food supplies and is one of the reasons for the great success of the order.

Typical diets of ungulate species include grasses, leaves, twigs, branches, seeds and fruits. Many species feed on a very restricted range of plants. Some are solely grazers, feeding only on grasses, while some are browsers, feeding mainly on leaves.

Members of this order have colonised nearly all of the available habitats in Africa.

A CHART TO SHOW BROAD CLASSIFICATION OF AFRICAN MAMMALS.

The chart is not intended to show evolutionary relationships.

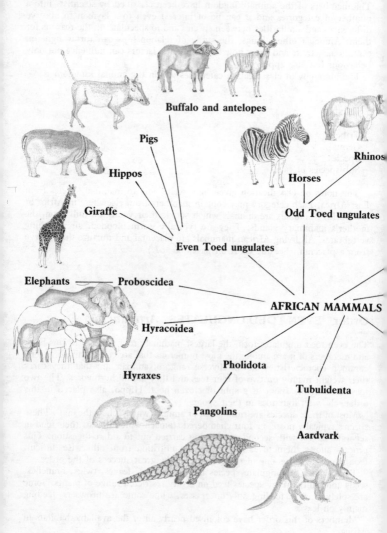

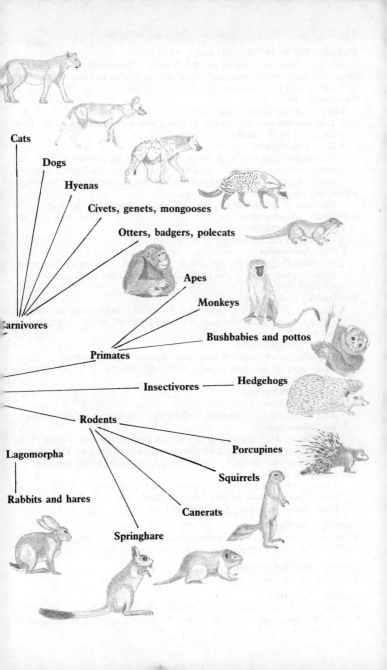

The order Even Toed Ungulates is subdivided as follows.

Family Bovidae Buffalo and Antelopes

Antelopes, unlike deer, possess horns which grow throughout the animal's life. Deer shed their antlers annually. There are no deer in tropical Africa; every deer-like animal is an antelope.

Sub-family Bovinae
 Tribe Bovini Ox-like mammals
  This includes only the buffalo in Africa which is a separate species from the Asian water buffalo.
 Tribe Tragelaphini
  The members of this tribe are visually related by patterns of body and throat markings and have twisted or spiral horns. The species included are eland, greater kudu, lesser kudu, bongo, nyala, sitatunga and bushbuck.

Sub-family Hippotragini
 Members of this group are roan and sable antelope and the oryx.

Sub-family Alcelaphinae
 Tribe Connochaetini
  This covers the wildebeest.
 Tribe Alcelaphini
  The Alcelaphines are the hartebeests. These are Lichtenstein's hartebeest, the con-specific Coke's and Jackson's hartebeest, the hirola and the tsessebe and topi.

Sub-family Reduncinae
 Members of this group are grazers associated with moist or wetland habitats. It includes waterbuck, the three reedbuck species, puku, lechwe and kob.

Sub-family Aepycerotinae
 The sole species included here is the impala which, although similar in some ways to gazelles, is sufficiently different for it to be classified separately.

Sub-family Antelopinae
 Tribe Antelopini
  This tribe covers the gazelles, Grant's and Thomson's, and the gerenuk.
 Tribe Neotragini
  These are smaller antelopes which have a more strongly developed use of facial and other scent-marking glands. Species included are klipspringer, oribi, steenbok, Sharpe's grysbok, dikdik, suni and pigmy antelope.

Sub-family Cephalophinae
 These are the duikers. Included here are yellow backed, Abbot's, common, Peter's, black fronted, white bellied, bay, red, Ruwenzori red, Natal red, red flanked, Zanzibar and blue.

Family Suidae Pigs

This family of visually similar animals includes giant forest hog, bushpig and warthog. Pigs have a simple stomach and are not ruminants.

Family Hippotamidae

From this region, the hippopotamus is the only member.

Family Giraffidae

The pattern of the giraffe's spoor confirms its membership of this order. Current thinking puts all giraffe into one species, *Giraffa camelopardalis*, although in the wild there seems not to be any hybridisation between, say, the reticulated and Masai races. This could be due to environmental rather than genetic reasons.

The okapi is the only other member of this family.

Order ODD TOED UNGULATES Perissodactyla

The odd toed ungulates are characterised by the fact that the animal's weight is carried on a main or central toe. The spoor shows as a single horseshoe hoof pattern of the zebras and the characteristic three-toed imprint of the rhinos. The order is divided into two families.

Family Equidae Horses
The two species of zebra are included in this family, Grevy's and Burchell's.

Family Rhinocerotidae
These are the white and black rhinos.

Order PROBOSCIDEA

Family Elephantidae
This unique group of 'long-nosed' animals has only one African member, the African elephant. Characteristic of the elephants are their elongated trunks, which are equipped with muscles and have evolved into a very useful fifth limb. It is a surprising fact that elephants walk on their toes, admittedly cushioned by a firm pad of flesh to spread out the load. The toes only show faintly in the spoor.

Order CARNIVORA Carnivores

As suggested by the name, many members of this order feed primarily on flesh, but this is far from exclusive. Some species are insectivorous and some vegetarian. The distinctions between some families are not at all obvious to the eye. For example, the dog-like hyenas are considered, from an evolutionary point of view, to be more closely related to the Viverridae family. The order is classified as follows.

Family Hyaenidae Hyenas
Sub-family Hyaeninae
  These are the true hyenas, characterised by powerful jaws and forequarters. The two species found here are the spotted and the striped.
Sub-family Protelinae
  The classification of the aardwolf has often been disputed but current thinking puts it here with the hyenas. Visually it is rather similar to the striped hyena but its feeding habits are quite different. It does not possess especially powerful jaws and has small teeth. It feeds almost exclusively on termites.

Family Canidae Dogs, jackals and foxes
These species are visually similar to dogs, differing mainly in size and colouration.

Sub-family Simocyoninae
The wild dog is placed here in a class of its own.

Sub-family Caninae
This includes the jackals, which are the most closely related to the domestic dog. Breeding between wild jackals and domestic dogs has been recorded. The species here are black backed, side striped and golden jackals.

Sub-family Otocyoninae
Worldwide, many foxes are placed in the Caninae sub-family, but the bat eared fox is considered different enough to merit its own.

Family Felidae Cats
Sub-family Felinae
All living cats are placed in this sub-family. As a group, cats are one of the most cohesive. They are visually similar, have very close behavioural similarities and basically similar diets. Differences in marking, from spots, rosettes and stripes to plain, are interesting, and probably result from behavioural differences and the need for camouflage in different habitats. All are carnivorous but the smaller members may sometimes also take insects. Their claws are normally retracted but can be extended at will. The cheetah is something of an exception in that its claws are not covered by a protective sheath when they are retracted.

Species included here are lion, leopard, cheetah, serval, caracal, golden cat and African wild cat.

Family Viverridae
Most of the members of this family have long sinuous bodies with long tails and muzzles and short legs. Some species are rather cat-like.

Sub-family Viverrinae
These are the animals that are commonly mistaken for true cats, which they are not. It includes the civet and the genets.

Sub-family Nandiniinae
The tree civet is placed here on its own.

Sub-family Herpestinae
These are the mongooses, a varied group of similarly shaped animals differing mainly in size. They have evolved to exploit a wide variety of habitats. The species included here are white tailed, large grey, marsh, Meller's, Selous', bushy tailed, slender, banded and dwarf.

Family Mustelidae
The members of this family are fierce, flesh-eating hunters.

Sub-family Lutrinae
These are the otters, species which are largely aquatic but spend some time on land. The two species covered here are the clawless and spotted necked.

Sub-family Mellivorinae
The honey badger is placed in this group on its own.

Sub-family Mustelinae
The two species here are the striped polecat and the striped weasel.

Order PRIMATES

This order is subdivided into two sub-orders, one accommodating the likes of bushbabies and the other including apes, monkeys and humans. Most species of this order are vegetarian but some, such as baboons, are omnivorous and will eat virtually anything. A large number of primates are associated with forests and may spend most, if not all of their lives in trees.

Sub-Order Anthropoidea
Family Pongidae
These are the great apes and species included here are the gorilla and chimpanzee. They do not have tails and spend at least part of their time on the ground.

Family Cercopithecidae
These are long-tailed monkeys and baboons. Species included are olive, yellow and chacma baboons, black and white and red colobus, Sykes' and blue monkeys, L'Hoest's, De Brazza's, vervet, white nosed, patas and black mangabey.

Sub-order Prosimii
Family Lorisidae
The bushbabies and potto are included in this family.

OTHER MAMMALS

A variety of mammals from different orders is included in this section. Their zoological classifications are as follows.

Order TUBULIDENTATA
Family Orycteropodidae
The unique aardvark is the only surviving member of this order. Although feeding solely on ants and termites, the aardvark possesses teeth, the purpose of which is unclear.

Order PHOLIDOTA
Family Manidae
The species of pangolins, also rather unusual animals, are placed here in their own order. Pangolins do not have teeth. They feed mainly on certain ant species.

Order RODENTIA

The rodents are one of the most successful orders on earth, having colonised just about every available habitat and niche with a wide variety of forms. The common characteristic of the order is an array of teeth adapted to gnawing.

Family Hystricidae
These are the porcupines, characterised by large size and spines on the back and tail.

Family Thryonomyidae
The two canerat species are included here.

Family Sciuridae
Of a large number of mainly arboreal squirrels in Africa, only the ground squirrels are included here. Tree squirrels are less commonly seen in many areas of East Africa.

Family Pedetidae
The springhare is placed here on its own. It is a rodent and not related to hares or rabbits.

Order LAGOMORPHA
Family Leporidae
These are the rabbits and hares.

Order HYRACOIDEA
Family Procavidae
The tree and rock hyraxes are included here in their own order. They are related in certain ways to the dugongs and elephants and used to be grouped with them in a single super-order.

Order INSECTIVORA
Family Erinaceidae
The hedgehog is one of the largest of the insectivores and is placed in a family of its own.

1.10 Checklist of species

UNGULATES
Buffalo and antelopes

Buffalo	78
Eland	79
Derby's eland	79
Greater kudu	80
Lesser kudu	81
Bongo	82
Nyala	83
Sitatunga	84
Bushbuck	85
Roan antelope	86
Sable antelople	87
Fringe eared oryx	88
Beisa oryx	88
Wildebeest	89
Coke's hartebeest	90
Jackson's hartebeest	90
Lichtenstein's hartebeest	91
Topi	92
Tsessebe	92
Hirola	93
Common waterbuck	94
Defassa waterbuck	94
Lechwe	95
Puku	96
Uganda kob	97
Bohor reedbuck	98
Mountain reedbuck	99
Southern reedbuck	100
Impala	101
Gerenuk	102
Grant's gazelle	103
Thomson's gazelle	104
Klipspringer	105
Oribi	106
Steenbok	107
Sharpe's grysbok	108
Kirk's dikdik	109
Guenther's dikdik	109
Suni	110
Pigmy antelope	110
Yellow backed duiker	111
Abbot's duiker	112
Common duiker	113

Peter's duiker	114
Black fronted duiker	115
White bellied duiker	116
Bay duiker	116
Red duiker	117
Ruwenzori red duiker	117
Natal red duiker	117
Red flanked duiker	118
Zanzibar duiker	119
Blue duiker	120

Pigs
Giant forest hog	121
Warthog	122
Bushpig	123

Hippopotamus
Hippopotamus	124

Giraffe
Common giraffe	125
Reticulated giraffe	126
Okapi	127

Zebra
Grevy's zebra	128
Common zebra	129

Rhinoceros
White rhinoceros	130
Black rhinoceros	131

ELEPHANT

African elephant	133

CARNIVORES

Hyenas
Spotted hyena	134
Striped hyena	135
Aardwolf	136

Dogs, Jackals and Foxes
Wild dog	137
Black backed jackal	138
Side striped jackal	139
Golden jackal	140
Bat eared fox	141

Cats and Cat-like Mammals
Lion	142
Leopard	143

Cheetah	144
Serval	145
Caracal	146
Golden cat	147
African wild cat	148
African civet	149
Tree civet	150
Large spotted genet	151
Small spotted genet	151

Mongooses

White tailed mongoose	152
Large grey mongoose	153
Marsh mongoose	154
Meller's mongoose	155
Selous' mongoose	156
Bushy tailed mongoose	157
Slender mongoose	158
Banded mongoose	159
Dwarf mongoose	160

Otters, Badgers and Weasels

Clawless otter	161
Spotted necked otter	161
Honey badger	162
Striped polecat	163
Striped weasel	163

PRIMATES

Apes

Mountain gorilla	164
Eastern lowland gorilla	164
Chimpanzee	165

Monkeys

Olive baboon	166
Yellow baboon	166
Chacma baboon	166
Sykes' monkey	167
Blue monkey	167
Golden monkey	167
L'Hoest's monkey	167
De Brazza's monkey	168
White nosed monkey	169
Vervet monkey	170
Patas monkey	171
Black and white colobus	172
Red colobus	173
Black mangabey	174

Bushbabies

| Potto | 175 |

Thick tailed bushbaby	176
Lesser bushbaby	177
Demidoff's bushbaby	177

OTHER MAMMALS

Aardvark	178
Pangolin	179
Porcupine	180
Greater canerat	181
Lesser canerat	181
Ground squirrel	182
Springhare	183
African hare	184
Scrub hare	184
Bunyoro rabbit	185
Red rock rabbit	185
Rock hyrax	186
Tree hyrax	187
Hedgehog	188

PART 2
The Mammals

ORDER **Even toed ungulates** Artiodactyla
FAMILY **Antelopes** Bovidae

BUFFALO *Syncerus caffer*
K: Mbogo, nyati F: Buffle D: Buffel

Photo: page 29

♂　　　　　　　　♀

Spoor
12 cm

Main colour	Shoulder height	Typical weight	Gestation period	Number of
Dark grey	1.4 m, 4'8"	750 kg, 1650 lb	340 days	young 1

Description
A large charcoal grey, cow-like animal related to the antelope. The wide curving horns are typical and the prominent ears hang low on the face. Females and young are more russet in colour and have generally smaller, less sweeping horns. A fully grown bull is a massive creature with a heavy solid central boss to the horns. The race which occurs in the forests to the west of the region is somewhat smaller with shorter, more swept back horns.

Habits
Buffalo congregate in herds which may be thousands strong in some areas but more typically number 50 – 100 animals. Older bulls become more solitary. Buffalo require water and move regularly between feeding grounds and water. They are grazers, active by day and night. A typical pose is with head thrown back and nostrils flared to catch an intruder's scent. A solid line-abreast of buffalo standing like this presents a formidable sight but for all their fearful reputation, a buffalo herd is very ready to stampede in panic at the least danger. A single lion in ambush by a river can prevent an entire herd from drinking. Under normal conditions, buffalo encountered on foot tend to flee rather than attack.

Habitat
Found in most habitats in Africa but often associated with wetlands and rank grasslands near water. They rest during the day in the shade of woodland trees or tall swamp grass.

Where best seen
Still reasonably common throughout its range and found in most of the parks and reserves of the region.

Distribution

ORDER **Even toed ungulates** Artiodactyla
FAMILY **Antelopes** Bovidae

ELAND *Taurotragus oryx*
DERBY'S ELAND *Taurotragus derbianus*
K: Pofu F: Elan D: Elanantilope

♂

Spoor
11 cm

Main colour	**Shoulder height**	**Typical weight**	**Gestation period**	**Number of**
Male: Grey	1.6 m, 5'4"	500 kg, 1100 lb	270 days	**young** 1
Female: Fawn				

Description
The most massive of the African antelopes, eland are a sandy tan in colour varying to a darker grey in old males. Relatively short but thick twisted horns are present in both sexes. A prominent dewlap hangs beneath the throat. There is a noticeable hump on the back and the body is patterned with delicate white striping. Females are smaller, more lightly built and russet in colour compared with males.

The rather larger Derby's eland has longer horns and a dewlap which starts under the chin. It occurs in central Africa as far east as Garamba in N.E. Zaïre.

Habits
Eland usually congregate in small herds of 10 – 30 animals. They are independent of water and tend to be much more mobile than other species, covering vast distances in their wanderings. They are quite shy and will often turn tail when encountered, setting off at a brisk trot until they disappear over the horizon. Eland sometimes make a high leap, over 2 m, often for no apparent reason. This presents a remarkable spectacle for so large a creature.

Eland are mainly browsers.

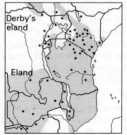

Distribution

Habitat
Savanna and light woodland. Dry thornbush, plains and mountain grassland. Found in most habitats except deserts, swamps and dense forest. Derby's eland are more closely associated with woodland.

Where best seen
Eland are not especially rare but they are thinly spread and not regularly encountered everywhere. Several herds are often present in Nairobi National Park.

ORDER **Even toed ungulates** Artiodactyla
FAMILY **Antelopes** Bovidae

GREATER KUDU *Tragelaphus strepsiceros*
K: Tandala F: Koudou D: Kudu **Photo:** page 30

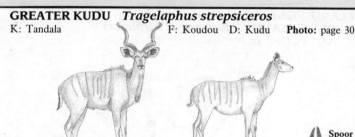

Spoor 10 cm

Main colour	Shoulder height	Typical weight	Gestation period	Number of young
Male: grey Female: russet	1.4 m, 4'7"	250 kg, 550 lb	210 days	1

Description
A large handsome antelope in shades of pale grey to dusky brown, the females being generally brown in colour. Males possess spectacular spiralled horns. Kudu are typical of the genus Tragelaphus in having narrow white stripes vertically down the body and along the spine. They are characteristically humped at the shoulder and possess a fringed dewlap of varying size beneath the throat.

Habits
Males are solitary or occur in small groups. Females and young, sometimes with one or more males, occur in larger groups of 6 – 20 animals. Kudu often stand quite still when disturbed and in spite of their size can be very difficult to see against a wooded background. They turn and flee, however, with little provocation, head thrown back to prevent the horns catching in the branches. Kudu are remarkably agile and can leap shoulder-high obstacles from standing. They become less shy when accustomed to visitors and when drought forces feeding and drinking away from cover.

Habitat
A woodland creature, typically of the miombo and mopane forest of central southern Africa. In the northern part of the region, tends to be confined to wooded hilly and mountainous districts. A browser feeding mainly on the leaves of certain shrubs and trees. Requires water but may go several days without drinking.

Where best seen
Rare in Kenya but often seen at Lake Bogoria. Much more common further south in reserves such as Ruaha and Selous as well as in Malaŵi and Zambia.

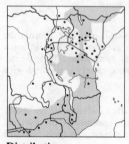

Distribution

ORDER **Even toed ungulates** Artiodactyla
FAMILY **Antelopes** Bovidae

LESSER KUDU *Strepsiceros imberbis*
K: Tandala ndogo   F: Petit koudou   D: Klein kudu

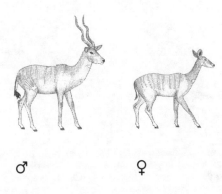

♂   ♀

 Spoor
7 cm

Main colour	Shoulder height	Typical weight	Gestation period	Number of young
Russet	1 m, 3'4"	105 kg, 230 lb	220 days	1

Description
A slender, more dainty version of the greater kudu. Coat colour is russet to grey, with a larger number of vertical stripes. Horns occur only in the male, spiralled but narrower than the greater kudu. There is a white chevron under the throat and at the base of the lower neck, as also occurs in the bushbuck and sitatunga. There is no fringe beneath the throat.

Habits
Lesser kudu are shy creatures which normally stay within the cover of thick thornbush scrub. They usually occur singly, in pairs or small family groups, and are browsers.

Habitat
Thick thornbush in relatively dry areas.

Where best seen
Not easy to see anywhere on account of their preference for thick bush. Reasonably common, however, in Meru and Kora, especially along the Tana River, and in parts of Tsavo as well as in northern Tanzania.

Distribution

ORDER **Even toed ungulates** Artiodactyla
FAMILY **Antelopes** Bovidae

BONGO *Boocercus euryceros*
K: Bongo, ndongoro   F: Bongo   D: Bongo

♂   ♀

Spoor 8 cm

Main colour	Shoulder height	Typical weight	Gestation period	Number of young
Russet	1.2 m, 4′	150 kg, 330 lb	285 days	1

Description
A handsome thickset antelope, rufous to orange in colour with thin white stripes vertically down the body. White chevrons are present on the face and throat. Horns are twisted, with a light spiral, and occur in both sexes.

Habits
Bongo are shy creatures and rarely seen. They are almost entirely nocturnal. They usually occur in small family groups.

Habitat
Dense mountain forest, especially bamboo, usually above 8000′ in altitude. They occur in lowland forest in central and west Africa.

Where best seen
Although bongo occur in several mountain areas of East Africa, they are rarely seen. They exist in Kenya on Mt Kenya, the Aberdares, the Mau escarpment and the Cherengani Hills. Also on forested mountains in southern Sudan and eastern Zaïre.

Distribution

ORDER **Even toed ungulates** Artiodactyla
FAMILY **Antelopes** Bovidae

NYALA *Tragelaphus angasii*
K: Nyala F: Nyala D: Tieflandnyala

♂ ♀ Spoor 6 cm

Main colour	Shoulder height	Typical weight	Gestation period	Number of
Male: grey brown	112 cm, 3'8"	110 kg, 240 lb	220 days	**young** 1
Female: russet				

Description
Nyala have the appearance of a shaggy-coated kudu with similar but less dramatically spiralled horns. They possess similar body stripes and males have a pattern of white spots on the flanks. Coat colour is grey to brown, with females and young tending to a paler fawn or russet. The legs of the male are distinctly orange. Males are rather larger than the females.

Habits
Nyala occur mainly in mixed family groups of around a dozen animals. They may also be encountered alone. Nyala are browsers, active during mornings and evenings.

Habitat
Thick thornbush scrub and dense woodland in low lying areas, with access to water.

Where best seen
Occurs within the region only in a restricted area on the Zambezi in southern Zambia and in southern Malaŵi. Easily seen and fairly numerous in Lengwe National Park.

Distribution

ORDER **Even toed ungulates** Artiodactyla
FAMILY **Antelopes** Bovidae

SITATUNGA *Tragelaphus spekei*
K: Nzohe F: Sitatunga D: Sumpfantilope   **Photo:** page 30

♂   Spoor
                                                   8 cm

Main colour	Shoulder height	Typical weight	Gestation period	Number of
Brown	90 cm, 3′	115 kg, 250 lb	225 days	young 1

Description
A shaggy coated brown to dark grey antelope of medium size. Twisted horns, a chevron between the eyes and white body stripes show the relationship to animals such as kudu and bushbuck. The markings vary regionally and in some areas the pattern does not show. Sitatunga have enormously elongated hooves to give support in their watery habitat.

Habits
Sitatunga are shy and retiring. They are largely nocturnal and hide during the day amid stands of papyrus. When disturbed, they may take to the water, with only the nostrils remaining visible.

Habitat
Dense stands of papyrus in and around suitable permanent wetlands.

Where best seen
Rarely seen unless deliberately sought. Saiv Swamp in Kenya offers the best opportunit Probably still common, however, around parts of Lakes Kyoga, Victoria, Tanganyika and Rukwa as well as in swampy areas of parks such as Akagera and Katavi.

Distribution

ORDER **Even toed ungulates** Artiodactyla
FAMILY **Antelopes** Bovidae

BUSHBUCK *Tragelaphus scriptus*
K: Pongo   F: Guib harnaché   D: Schirrantilope

Main colour	Shoulder height	Typical weight	Gestation period	Number of young
Russet	75 cm, 2'6"	35 kg, 75 lb	180 days	1

Spoor 4 cm

Description
A small golden tan antelope with prominent ears and large appealing eyes. Males develop horns which in older animals show a twist. The coat pattern varies regionally but typically has delicate stripes and dots scattered over the body and flanks, especially in the male. Bushbuck in the northern part of the region tend not to be so well marked and may be completely plain. Older males become darker in colour, sometimes tending almost to black. The white throat mark and dark 'harness' around the neck are also characteristic, although other species of the Tragelaphus genus share certain features of the bushbuck's patterning.

Habits
A shy little creature which spends much of its time hidden amid dense foliage, emerging at dusk or during the night. Bushbuck are browsers and still common throughout much of their range on account of their retiring habits. They occur singly, in pairs and in small groups where they are numerous.

Distribution

Habitat
Moist forested areas including mountain moorland, lakeside and riverine woodland.

Where best seen
May be glimpsed in suitable locations throughout the range. Especially numerous in the Aberdares salient.

| ORDER | **Even toed ungulates** Artiodactyla |
| FAMILY | **Antelopes** Bovidae |

ROAN ANTELOPE *Hippotragus equinus*
K: Korongo F: Hippotrague D: Pferdeantilope

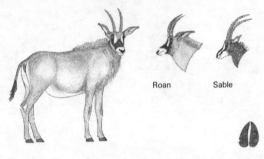

Roan   Sable

Spoor
10 cm

Main colour	Shoulder height	Typical weight	Gestation period	Number of young
Fawn	1.4 m, 4'6"	270 kg, 600 lb	280 days	1

Description
A large, horse-like antelope coloured sandy fawn with a very distinctive black and white facial pattern. Both sexes possess horns, those of the male being thicker and more arched but less so than those of the sable. Roan have a thick mane and a shaggy fringe on the throat. Noticeably tufted ears are a characteristic feature. Coat colour varies regionally from a light sandy colour to a rufous tan.

Habits
Roan are primarily grazers, occurring in small herds or family groups of typically 6 – 10 animals. They may also be encountered in pairs or as solitary animals. They do not as a rule mix with other species. Roan are nervous and not easily approached.

Habitat
Roan require regular access to water and are generally associated with dry woodland areas where there are rivers or waterholes. This habitat preference limits their distribution in much of East Africa.

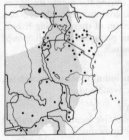

Where best seen
An endangered species that is spread thinly throughout much of sub-Saharan Africa where there is suitable habitat. Most likely seen in the wooded reserves of southern Tanzania and Zambia but also encountered in Shimba Hills and Ruma in Kenya.

Distribution

ORDER **Even toed ungulates** Artiodactyla
FAMILY **Antelopes** Bovidae

SABLE ANTELOPE *Hippotragus niger*
K: Pala hala F: Hippotrague noir D: Rappenantilope **Photo:** pages 35, 31

♂

♀

Spoor
9 cm

Main colour	Shoulder height	Typical weight	Gestation period	Number of
Male: black	1.35 m, 4'6"	230 kg, 500 lb	245 days	**young** 1
Female: russet				

Description
A large chestnut brown or black antelope with sturdy, backward curving horns in both sexes. Breeding age males are black with huge arching horns. The black and white facial pattern is distinctive and quite different from that of the roan (sable has white cheeks, not nose). White underparts and a thick mane are also noticeable. Sable are slightly smaller and lighter than roan.

Habits
Sable gather in herds of 20 – 30 animals. A herd may consist of females and young under a dominant male, or of non-breeding males only. Older males become more solitary. Sable are often encountered standing in the shade of tall trees chewing the cud in cattle-like fashion. They are primarily grazers and are dependent on water, usually coming to drink in the hotter hours of the day.

Habitat
A creature of dry open woodlands where it can graze in grassy clearings or adjacent savanna. Often seen close to rivers, especially during dry seasons.

Where best seen
Nowhere numerous in East Africa and, on account of its habitat preference, difficult to observe closely. More common in the wooded reserves of Malawi, Zambia and southern Tanzania. Also may be seen in Shimba Hills in Kenya.

Distribution

ORDER **Even toed ungulates** Artiodactyla
FAMILY **Antelopes** Bovidae

ORYX *Oryx gazella*
K: Choroa   F: Oryx   D: Spiessbock   **Photo:** page 31, 32

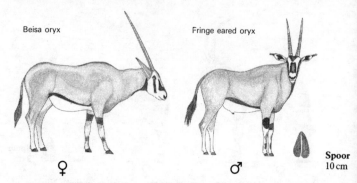

Beisa oryx

Fringe eared oryx

Spoor
10 cm

♀   ♂

Main colour	Shoulder height	Typical weight	Gestation period	Number of young
Pale grey	1.2 m, 4'	220 kg, 480 lb	260 days	1

Description
A large antelope with long straight horns in both sexes. Colouring is an ashy pink to pale grey with distinct black markings on the face, legs and body. Young oryx are more chestnut coloured. The fringe eared oryx differs from the beisa in having noticeable black tufts at the tips of its ears. It occurs south of the Tana River while the beisa oryx is found in the arid areas to the north.

Habits
A grazer of dry and semi-desert areas, gathering in herds of up to 80 animals. More usually seen in herds of 15 – 25, and solitary males or pairs may also be encountered. A breeding herd consists of a male with a harem of females and young. This species is not dependent on water but will drink and indeed stay close to water if it is available. In desert areas, long distances may be covered in search of grazing and water. Oryx are normally placid animals but are well able to defend themselves against predators using their spear-like horns.

Distribution

Habitat
Dry savanna and semi-desert. The beisa oryx is able to survive in almost totally arid areas while the region inhabited by the fringe eared oryx includes more thornbush scrub and grasslands.

Where best seen
Beisa oryx: Samburu and Meru and much of northern Kenya.
Fringe eared oryx: Amboseli, Tsavo and the drier parts of northern Tanzania.

ORDER **Even toed ungulates** Artiodactyla
FAMILY **Antelopes** Bovidae

WILDEBEEST or GNU *Connochaetes taurinus*
K: Nyumbu F: Gnou D: Gnu **Photo:** page 32

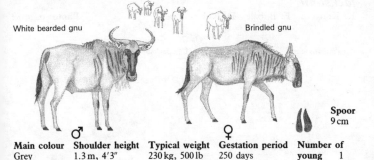

White bearded gnu

Brindled gnu

Spoor
9 cm

Main colour	Shoulder height	Typical weight	Gestation period	Number of
Grey	1.3 m, 4'3"	230 kg, 500 lb	250 days	young 1

Description
A smoky to charcoal grey antelope with a bony cattle-like head and horns and a long swishing tail. The sexes are similar. There are two sub-species in the region. The white bearded gnu has a pale shaggy fringe on the throat. The brindled gnu, or blue wildebeest, lacks this but is more clearly streaked down the forepart of the body.

Habits
Wildebeest are gregarious, occurring in herds that may be thousands strong during dry season concentrations and migrations. They are water-dependent grazers. Herds follow in each other's footsteps leaving narrow beaten pathways that meander across the plains. The lack of a dominant leader is apparent in much aimless crossing and recrossing of rivers while migrating. Animals keep in touch with a sheep-like bleating. The alarm call is a nasal snort. Wildebeest are the preferred prey of lion in many areas on account of their abundance and relative ease of capture. Herds of the blue wildebeest tend to be much smaller than those of the white bearded gnu.

Distribution

Habitat
The white bearded gnu inhabits open grassy plains while the blue wildebeest, which occurs south of the Rufiji river in Tanzania, is a species of open woodlands and adjacent savanna.

Where best seen
Occurs in most of the savanna parks of the region. Most spectacular during the annual migrations in Serengeti and Mara. These occur between August and October depending on rainfall patterns. Large dry season concentrations also in Nairobi and Amboseli.

ORDER **Even toed ungulates** Artiodactyla
FAMILY **Antelopes** Bovidae

COKE'S HARTEBEEST *Alcelaphus buselaphus cokii*
JACKSON'S HARTEBEEST *Alcelaphus buselaphus jacksonii*
K: Kongoni F: Bubale D: Kuhantilope   Photo: page 33

Coke's hartebeest

Jackson's hartebeest

Spoor
7 cm

Main colour	Shoulder height	Typical weight	Gestation period	Number of
Sandy	1.2 m, 4'	150 kg, 330 lb	240 days	young 1

Description
Hartebeest are large ungainly antelope with a rapid bouncing gait. The horns, which are present in both sexes, protrude directly from a pedicle of bone on top of the head. The body seems to slope down towards the hindquarters. Coke's hartebeest, commonly called kongoni, is a pale sandy colour with horns spread out and kinked vertically. Jackson's hartebeest is considered to be the same species but has a quite different appearance with the horns kinked backwards. It is darker in colour than Coke's hartebeest.

Habits
Hartebeest are grazers but largely independent of water. They gather in family groups or small herds up to about 30 animals but may congregate in larger groups during wet season migrations. Generally less migratory than wildebeest, however. Early explorers found hartebeest amongst the most numerous of plains game but they are rather less common now.

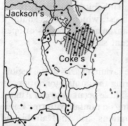
Distribution

Habitat
Open grassy plains and light woodland.

Where best seen
Spread throughout their range but rather localised. Coke's hartebeest is often encountered in the plains areas of Kenya and northern Tanzania and has become resident in Nairobi National Park. Jackson's hartebeest occurs in western Kenya and Uganda.

ORDER **Even toed ungulates** Artiodactyla
FAMILY **Antelopes** Bovidae

LICHTENSTEIN'S HARTEBEEST *Alcelaphus lichtensteinii*
K: Kongoni F: Bubale D: Kuhantilope

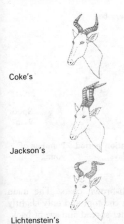

Coke's

Jackson's

Lichtenstein's

Spoor
8 cm

Main colour	Shoulder height	Typical weight	Gestation period	Number of young
Chestnut	1.25 m, 4'2'''	170 kg, 375 lb	240 days	1

Description
This hartebeest species is reddish brown, the horns narrower than in the kongoni and kinked sharply backwards. It is rather similar in appearance to Jackson's hartebeest but a little larger. The pedicle is less marked on Lichtenstein's hartebeest, which also has distinctive black knee markings on the forelegs. A bare elliptical patch behind the shoulder, caused by rubbing with the horns, is sometimes present.

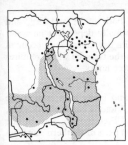

Distribution

Habits
These hartebeest are grazers, largely independent of water. They also gather in small herds.

Habitat
Grassy plains and woodland, with Lichtenstein's hartebeest preferring a more wooded environment than other hartebeest species.

Where best seen
Rather locally distributed in the southern part of the region where woodlands predominate.

ORDER **Even toed ungulates** Artiodactyla
FAMILY **Antelopes** Bovidae

TOPI and TSESSEBE *Damaliscus lunatus*
K: Nyamera   F: Damalisque   D: Leier

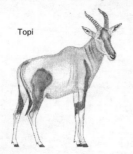

Spoor
9 cm

Main colour	Shoulder height	Typical weight	Gestation period	Number of young
Chestnut	1.25 m, 4'2"	140 kg, 300 lb	240 days	1

Description
Medium to large antelope with sleek rich reddish-brown coats. The main difference is in horn shape which is almost lyrate in the topi and only slightly backward curving. The horns of the tsessebe are wider spread and swept back. The sexes are similar. There are distinctive black markings on the legs and thighs and the lower parts of the legs are orange in colour. A further subspecies called the tiang is very similar to the topi and occurs in eastern and northern Kenya.

Habits
A grazer of savanna plains occurring in small herds, often alongside other plains species such as wildebeest and zebra. They are related to the hartebeest and possess the same bouncing run. The tsessebe, however, can gallop like a trained race-horse and is reputed to be the fastest of all antelope. Topi have a typical posture, standing on a raised mound or termite hill from where they can act as sentries for the herd.

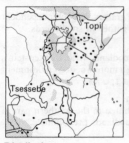

Distribution

Habitat
Savanna grasslands, both moist and dry, and open woodlands. Normally dependent on water but often seen in quite dry areas. Topi occur in more open areas than the tsessebe which requires shade during the hotter hours.

Where best seen
Topi are numerous and easily seen around the southern part of Lake Victoria including Akagera, Serengeti and Mara. Tsessebe are rare in the region but still occur in parts of southern Tanzania and Zambia.

ORDER **Even toed ungulates** Artiodactyla
FAMILY **Antelopes** Bovidae

HIROLA or HUNTER'S HARTEBEEST
Damaliscus hunteri
K: Hirola   F: Hirola   D: Hirola

Main colour	Shoulder height	Typical weight	Gestation period	Number of
Sandy	1.1 m, 3'8"	110 kg, 240 lb	240 days	young 1

Description
Similar in colouring and general shape to Coke's hartebeest but a little smaller and without an obvious horn pedicle on the head. The horns are quite different, being almost vertical and lyrate, rather like those of the impala. There is a characteristic white chevron between the eyes and the tail is white, not black as in other hartebeest species.

Habits
Hirola are a rare species confined to a handful of localities in north eastern Kenya. They occur in small herds and are primarily grazers.

Habitat
Semi-desert savanna and thornbush. Although creatures of arid areas, they migrate towards the Tana River during periods of harsh drought.

Where best seen
To all intents and purposes, confined to the Arawale reserve in Kenya.

Distribution

ORDER **Even toed ungulates** Artiodactyla
FAMILY **Antelopes** Bovidae

WATERBUCK *Kobus ellipsyprymnus*
K: Kuru   F: Kob   D: Wasserbock   **Photo:** page 34

Ringed waterbuck   Defassa waterbuck
♂   ♀

Spoor
8 cm

Main colour	Shoulder height	Typical weight	Gestation period	Number of
Brown	1.3 m, 4'3"	240 kg, 530 lb	280 days	young 1

Description
A thickset, deer-like antelope with a shaggy brown coat varying regionally from fawn to chocolate. Males possess horns which are stout but elegantly lyrate. Common waterbuck, also called ringed waterbuck, have a distinct white ring around the rump whilst the defassa has a white patch in the same place. Intermediate forms appear to exist where the two sub-species overlap.

Habits
Most often seen in small groups of females and young with one or more males. Herd size typically 5 – 30 though usually 5 – 10. Waterbuck remain within a relatively small territory and are less shy than many other species. When they do flee, it is with a bounding gait that takes them crashing through thick undergrowth. They are preyed upon by lion, but only in the absence of other preferred species, the flesh apparently having a rank flavour.

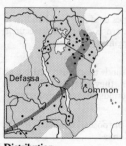
Distribution

Habitat
A grazer of rank herbage in the immediate vicinity of rivers, swamps and lakes. Found away from open water in areas such as mountain moorlands that are generally moist.

Where best seen
Almost anywhere within the range where there is open water and dense bush or woodland. Those at Lake Nakuru have bred prolifically and can be seen in herds of over 50. The Rift Valley forms a fairly clear dividing line between the two races and intermediate forms may be found in this area in such places as Arusha and Lake Manyara.

ORDER **Even toed ungulates** Artiodactyla
FAMILY **Antelopes** Bovidae

LECHWE *Kobus leche*
K: Lechwe   F: Kob lechwe   D: Litschi   **Photo:** page 35

Red lechwe

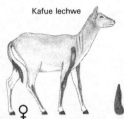
Kafue lechwe

Spoor
7 cm

Main colour	**Shoulder height** ♂	**Typical weight** ♀	**Gestation period**	**Number of young**
Fawn	1 m, 3'3"	100 kg, 220 lb	225 days	1

Description
A medium-sized antelope with a glowing, slightly furry, apricot-hued coat. The belly is white. Powerful hindquarters and, in the male, beautifully swept horns are the key identifiers. As with many species, it may often be the stance, behaviour and habitat that allow identification rather than distinctive features. Female lechwe may otherwise be mistaken by a casual observer for puku, reedbuck, impala or even bushbuck, all of which occur in similar localities. There is a black streak on the front of the forelegs in the lechwe. This is especially marked in the Kafue lechwe. The black lechwe has darker sides and face. The red lechwe is more even in tone.

Habits
Lechwe graze in small herds on floodplains along certain rivers and around swamps and lakes. A breeding herd may consist of up to 30 females and young with a dominant male. Non-breeding herds numbering hundreds of animals may be seen at some seasons. Mature males may be encountered singly, in pairs or in small groups. Lechwe are very agile in shallow water and progress in a series of bounding leaps when disturbed.

Distribution

Habitat
Floodplains. Lechwe are at home in riverside, lakeside and swamp edge environments. They are unhappy on dry ground. Because of this dependence on a restricted habitat, and because of threats to the continued existence of these habitats, lechwe are considered an endangered

Where best seen
Kafue lechwe: Kafue.
Black lechwe: Lochinvar.
Red lechwe: on the Zambezi where it forms the boundary with the Caprivi Strip of Namibia.

ORDER **Even toed ungulates** Artiodactyla
FAMILY **Antelopes** Bovidae

PUKU *Kobus vardonii*
K: Puku   F: Puku   D: Puku

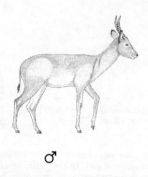

♂

Spoor
6 cm

Main colour	Shoulder height	Typical weight	Gestation period	Number of young
Fawn	90 cm, 3′	70 kg, 150 lb	240 days	1

Description
The puku is a medium-sized antelope with a russet coat. There are no distinguishing features such as dark leg markings as in reedbuck and the belly is less pale than in the lechwe. Males possess horns which are ridged and semi-lyrate but relatively short.

Habits
Puku are grazers, occurring in small herds or family groups of up to 15 animals. Puku are rarely found far from their preferred habitat close to water.

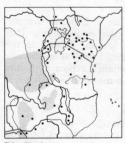

Habitat
Grassy plains and lightly wooded savanna close to rivers, lakes and swamps, river banks and seasonally inundated floodplains.

Where best seen
Puku must count as rare, especially in East Africa where they occur only in southern Tanzania in Katavi, on Lakes Tanganyika, Rukwa and Malaŵi and between the Great Ruaha and Kilombero rivers. More widespread and numerous in Zaïre and Zambia.

Distribution

ORDER **Even toed ungulates** Artiodactyla
FAMILY **Antelopes** Bovidae

UGANDA KOB *Adenota kob*
K: Ensumu   F: Kob de Buffon   D: Grasantilope

♂

Spoor
6 cm

Main colour	Shoulder height	Typical weight	Gestation period	Number of
Fawn	90 cm, 3'	60 kg, 130 lb	265 days	young 1

Description
The kob is rather similar to the puku. Coat colour is an even fawn. Males have horns which are intermediate in shape and length between those of the puku and the impala. A white ring around the eye and black markings on the forelegs are characteristic features.

Habits
Kob are grazers which occur normally in small herds or family groups, although single non-breeding males are sometimes encountered. Kob are highly territorial, defending relatively small areas against competition from intrusive males. This behaviour is less marked since the large herds have been seriously depleted in western Uganda.

Habitat
Grassy plains, usually close to water.

Where best seen
Restricted distribution but still regularly seen in Kabalega, Ruwenzori and Virunga.

Distribution

ORDER **Even toed ungulates** Artiodactyla
FAMILY **Antelopes** Bovidae

BOHOR REEDBUCK *Redunca redunca*
K: Tohe   F: Redunca   D: Gemeine riedbock

Photo: page 34

♂

Spoor
5 cm

Main colour	Shoulder height	Typical weight	Gestation period	Number of young
Fawn	70 cm, 2'4"	35 kg, 80 lb	220 days	1

Description
The three reedbuck species are distinctive in having forward curved horns in the male and a dark glandular spot at the side of the neck. There are dark markings down the front of the forelegs. The bohor reedbuck is the middle-sized of the three, its coat colour an attractive golden fawn.

Habits
Reedbuck generally occur in small groups of 6 – 10 animals. They frequent areas alongside water where rank herbage allows concealment. Reedbuck flee with an upraised tail revealing a white patch beneath. They hide in open grassland by crouching to the ground.

Habitat
Marshy and moist grassy areas by rivers and lakes, especially where there is tall grass cover. Bohor reedbuck also occur on some mountains which can lead to confusion with the mountain reedbuck.

Where best seen
Lake Nakuru and other lakes and rivers in Kenya and northern Tanzania.

Distribution

ORDER **Even toed ungulates** Artiodactyla
FAMILY **Antelopes** Bovidae

MOUNTAIN REEDBUCK *Redunca fulvorufula*
K: Tohe ya milima   F: Redunca de montagne   D: Bergriedbock

♂

Spoor
5 cm

Main colour	Shoulder height	Typical weight	Gestation period	Number of young
Grey brown	70 cm, 2'4"	30 kg, 65 lb	210 days	1

Description
Similar in general appearance to the bohor reedbuck but the colouring is rather greyer, especially on the sides and flanks. The belly is a contrasting white. The eyes in this species appear to be more prominent. Forward curved horns and black neck spot are present. Female reedbuck do not possess horns.

Habits
Like the bohor reedbuck, they occur in small groups and are found in grassy areas where there is also cover.

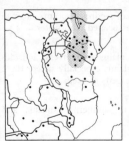

Habitat
The mountain reedbuck has a discontinuous distribution occurring where there is suitable highland terrain. They prefer grassy slopes, often where there are rocky outcrops and some bush cover. They require access to water.

Where best seen
Not often identified with certainty in the parks of the region, especially as both mountain and bohor reedbuck occur in the same localities in some areas. Occurs on the Nyika plateau in Malaŵi.

Distribution

ORDER **Even toed ungulates** Artiodactyla
FAMILY **Antelopes** Bovidae

SOUTHERN REEDBUCK *Redunca arundinum*
K: Tohe ya kusina   F: Redunca grande   D: Grossriedbock

♂

Spoor
6 cm

Main colour	Shoulder height	Typical weight	Gestation period	Number of
Fawn	85 cm, 2'7"	75 kg, 165 lb	225 days	**young** 1

Description
The largest of the reedbuck, with wider spread but still forward curving horns. The southern reedbuck is paler in colour than the bohor, varying from golden tan to greyish brown. Dark streaks are present on the forelegs. The alternative name of common reedbuck is hardly appropriate in this region as the species only becomes truly common further south in Africa.

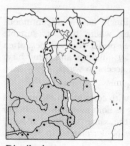

Distribution

Habits
As the other species of reedbuck, occurs in small groups. Invariably associated with water.

Habitat
Lakeshores, grassy plains near rivers, hillsides and mountain moorland, especially where there is tall grass cover or beds of reeds.

Where best seen
Suitable locations in southern Tanzania and Zambia.

ORDER **Even toed ungulates** Artiodactyla
FAMILY **Antelopes** Bovidae

IMPALA *Aepyceros melampus*
K: Swala pala   F: Pallah   D: Schwarzfersenantilope   **Photo:** page 36

♂   ♀   **Spoor** 6 cm

Main colour	Shoulder height	Typical weight	Gestation period	Number of young
Fawn	90 cm, 3′	50 kg, 110 lb	195 days	1

Description
A common, medium-sized antelope in shades of pale tan. The male possesses lyrate horns which are both beautiful and characteristic. The coat is banded horizontally, darker on the back and white underneath. Females have elongated faces which once noted differentiate the species from other similar antelope with which they may be confused at first sight.

Habits
A gregarious antelope occurring in herds of up to 30 or more. Herds may be all young males or a harem of females and young under a single dominant male. Basic herd types may co-exist alongside each other, resulting in large agglomerations of impala. Impala are mainly browsers but also graze. When competing for leadership of a herd, males chase each other frantically in circles and figures of eight. A fearful lion-like roaring is emitted by males during the rut. Females indulge in huge flying leaps with tail raised to show a white fluffy patch beneath. Similarly impressive leaps form the usual escape from predators.

Distribution

Habitat
Primarily light woodland adjacent to savanna, rivers, lakes and swamps. Although most often found close to water, impala are not always reliant on it and occur in some very dry areas.

Where best seen
One of the most widespread and easily seen of antelopes. Very common in most of the savanna reserves of the region.

ORDER **Even toed ungulates** Artiodactyla
FAMILY **Antelopes** Bovidae

GERENUK *Litocranius walleri*
K: Swala twiga F: Gazelle de Waller D: Giraffengazelle **Photo:** page 36, 43

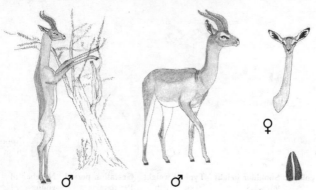

Main colour	Shoulder height	Typical weight	Gestation period	Number of
Fawn	95 cm, 3'2"	50 kg, 110 lb	205 days	**young** 1

Description
A unique long-necked antelope. Gerenuk are coloured in broad bands of pale fawn, with a white belly like gazelle and impala, but the elongated neck renders them immediately identifiable. Very large ears for the size of head are notable especially in the hornless female. The gerenuk is at the same time extraordinarily elegant yet in some ways rather ungainly. It is has some similarity to the dibatag which occurs in Somalia.

Habits
Gerenuk are encountered singly, in pairs or in small family groups. They browse during the day and have an unusual habit of rising daintily on to their hind legs in order to feed higher up than competing browsers such as impala or dikdik. Gerenuk tend to move quite slowly as the balance of the neck hinders rapid progress but they are able to put on a tremendous turn of speed and leap like impala when pursued by predators such as cheetah.

Habitat
A species of dry thornbush country, not dependent on water.

Where best seen
Samburu and Meru. Also the northern part of Amboseli and in many unprotected areas of thornbush scrub in northern Tanzania, east and northern Kenya.

Distribution

ORDER	**Even toed ungulates** Artiodactyla
FAMILY	**Antelopes** Bovidae

GRANT'S GAZELLE *Gazella grantii*
K: Swala granti F: Gazelle de Grant D: Grantgazelle   **Photo:** page 37, 43

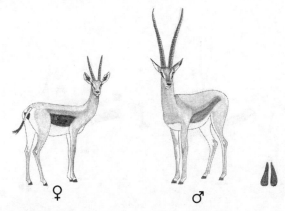

Main colour	Shoulder height	Typical weight	Number of young
Fawn	85 cm, 2'9"	70 kg, 155 lb	1

Description
The larger of the two gazelle of this region. A stocky but graceful animal with a silky coat subtly banded in shades of fawn but faintly pinkish in comparison to other antelopes. The darker lateral stripe is often more pronounced in the female but less clear than in Thomson's gazelle. The belly is white. Both sexes have horns, those of the male being very much longer and stouter. They vary in shape regionally from almost parallel to widely diverging. Horn-shape is used as a basis for identifying a number of sub-species within the region. Grant's gazelle is reckoned to possess the largest horns for its body size of any African antelope. These animals have a very alert, upright stance.

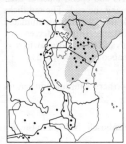

Distribution

Habits
Grant's gazelle occur in small herds of mixed or single sex. They have a trotting gait when moving. They are grazers, associated with the typical plains of East Africa, but do not migrate like Thomson's gazelle and are less dependent on water.

Habitat
Open savanna grasslands, especially in drier areas.

Where best seen
May be encountered in most of the drier areas of savanna parks in Kenya and Tanzania and in many places in between.

ORDER **Even toed ungulates** Artiodactyla
FAMILY **Antelopes** Bovidae

THOMSON'S GAZELLE *Gazella thomsonii*
K: Swala tomi F: Gazelle de Thomson D: Thomsongazelle **Photo:** page 44

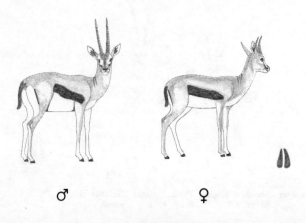

♂　　　　　　　　♀

Main colour	Shoulder height	Typical weight	Gestation period	Number of young
Fawn	65 cm, 2'2"	27 kg, 60 lb	190 days	1

Description
A small thickset gazelle coloured golden fawn with sharpy defined black and white bands along the lower part of the body. Males possess long horns for their size but those of the females are little more than wispy prongs.

Habits
'Tommies' gather in very large herds, thousands strong during migrations and dry season concentrations. They are daytime grazers and spend most of their time feeding and chewing the cud. The tail flicks characteristically back and forth like an animated fly-whisk. Thomson's gazelle are the preferred prey of cheetah in some areas and newly born fawns may be taken by eagles, baboons and leopards.

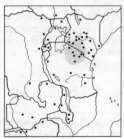

Habitat
Short grass plains in northern Tanzania and central southern Kenya.

Where best seen
Serengeti, Mara and Amboseli. Nairobi in the dry season.

Distribution

ORDER **Even toed ungulates** Artiodactyla
FAMILY **Antelopes** Bovidae

KLIPSPRINGER *Oreotragus oreotragus*
K: Mbuzi mawe   F: Oréotrague   D: Klipspringer

Spoor
1.5 cm

Main colour	Shoulder height	Typical weight	Gestation period	Number of
Grey brown	60 cm, 2′	12 kg, 25 lb	215 days	**young** 1

Description
A small yellowish-grey antelope with a curiously alert expression. Raised hooves give an impression of walking on tiptoe. The horns are short and spiky. Female klipspringer tend to be slightly larger than the males and are usually, but not always, hornless.

Habits
Klipspringer are nearly always associated with rocky hillsides and they clamber with ease over steep rocky cliffs where they can escape detection. They are shy and easily put to flight but often stand still for a second or two before disappearing. Klipspringer are usually seen alone or in twos or threes. They are browsers, largely independent of water.

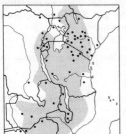

Distribution

Habitat
Confined to rocky outcrops, broken hilly terrain and koppies, especially where there is some growth of shrubs.

Where best seen
Discontinuously spread but not uncommon throughout the range wherever suitable outcrops occur.

ORDER **Even toed ungulates** Artiodactyla
FAMILY **Antelopes** Bovidae

ORIBI *Ourebia ourebi*
K: Taya   F: Ourébie   D: Bleichböckchen

♀

Spoor
3 cm

Main colour	Shoulder height	Typical weight	Gestation period	Number of
Fawn	60 cm, 2′	15 kg, 33 lb	210 days	young 1

Description
A small golden-tan antelope with a characteristic black hairless patch at the base of the ear. The black fluffy tail is also distinctive. Males possess short straight horns. Oribi are smaller and more upright in posture than reedbuck and larger than steenbok.

Habits
Oribi are most often encountered alone but may also be found in small family

groups. In areas where they are common, they are not especially shy and feed in quite open grassy areas. They are diurnal.

Habitat
The moister, more verdant areas of grassy savanna and open woodland.

Where best seen
Common in some areas but strangely absent from other apparently suitable places. Akagera and Ruma offer the best chances in the region.

Distribution

| ORDER | **Even toed ungulates** Artiodactyla |
| FAMILY | **Antelopes** Bovidae |

STEENBOK *Raphicerus campestris*
K: Funo, tondoro   F: Steenbok   D: Steinböckchen   **Photo:** page 44

Spoor
3 cm

Main colour	Shoulder height	Typical weight	Gestation period	Number of young
Fawn	52 cm, 1'8"	12 kg, 26 lb	170 days	1

Description
A very small antelope with disproportionately enormous ears. The coat is a golden tan colour. Males have short spiky horns. In comparison, common duiker have a black face and are greyer, while oribi are larger and have a black spot on the neck. Sharpe's grysbok has a furrier appearance and dikdik are much greyer in colour. When disturbed, steenbok have an alert upright posture. Not to be confused with steinbok which is a European animal found in the Alps.

Habits
A shy creature with a rapid scampering flight. Steenbok hide easily by flattening themselves to the ground and folding their ears back. They often pause in flight to glance back at an intruder, when the characteristic ears may be seen. They browse and graze but are not dependent on water. Steenbok occur as solitary animals or in pairs. They are active by day.

Habitat
Typically a creature of dry savanna and semi-desert plains. More widespread and common further south in Africa.

Where best seen
Dry scrub savanna in many of the parks of southern Kenya and northern Tanzania.

Distribution

| ORDER | **Even toed angulates** Artiodactyla |
| FAMILY | **Antelopes** Bovidae |

SHARPE'S GRYSBOK *Raphicerus sharpei*
K: Funo   F: Grysbok de Sharpe   D: Sharpe greisbock

♀

Spoor
2.5 cm

Main colour	Shoulder height	Typical weight	Gestation period	Number of young
Fawn	45 cm, 1'6"	11 kg, 24 lb	210 days	1

Description
Very like the closely related steenbok in size and shape but colouring is rather redder with the body speckled with white flecks. The male has short horns. The ears, although prominent, are smaller than those of the steenbok.

Distribution

Habits
A shy, secretive creature that is rarely seen. Sharpe's grysbok are primarily nocturnal and occur in pairs or alone. They feed mainly by browsing but do also graze.

Habitat
Low scrub, secondary growth and grassy areas where there is some cover and woodlands with light undergrowth.

Where best seen
Rarely encountered anywhere in the region as they lie concealed unless approached very closely. Probably not uncommon in suitable areas.

ORDER **Even toed ungulates** Artiodactyla
FAMILY **Antelopes** Bovidae

DIKDIK *Madoqua kirkii, Madoqua guentheri*
K: Dikidiki   F: Dik-dik   D: Dikdik

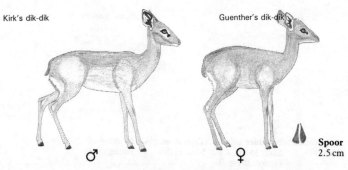

Spoor 2.5 cm

Main colour	Shoulder height	Typical weight	Gestation period	Number of young
Grey	40 cm, 1'4"	5 kg, 11 lb	180 days	1

Description
The two species of dikdik are amongst the smallest of antelope. They are a sandy grey in colour with the legs tinged orange. The snout is characteristically elongated, more so in Guenther's dikdik than in Kirk's. Guenther's dikdik is the larger species and is a more even grey in colour. Hybrids may occur in the areas where the two species overlap. Males have short straight horns but both sexes have a short tuft of hair on the crown. All dikdik possess black glandular markings immediately forward of the eye.

Habits
Dikdik are browsers of low thornbush though they will also feed on grass shoots. They are diurnal and although shy can be approached quite closely in some areas. They often occur in pairs or family groups.

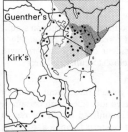

Distribution

Habitat
Dense thornbush scrub and woodland with thick undergrowth especially in dry areas. They also occur in scrub along rivers and drainage lines along which they may penetrate into otherwise unsuitable areas. Guenther's dikdik, which is found in northern Kenya, is more associated with arid regions.

Where best seen
Quite often encountered in many of the parks of the region where there is suitable dry scrub.

ORDER **Even toed ungulates** Artiodactyla
FAMILY **Antelopes** Bovidae

SUNI *Neotragus moschatus*
PIGMY ANTELOPE *Neotragus batesi*
K: Paa, suni F: Antelope musquée D: Moschusböckchen

Spoor 2 cm

Main colour	Shoulder height	Typical weight	Number of young
Fawn	Suni: 35 cm, 1'1'' Pigmy: 30 cm, 1'	5 kg, 11 lb	1

Description
These are among the smallest antelope of the region and indeed the pigmy antelope is one of the smallest in the African continent. The suni is not unlike a dikdik but it lacks the elongated snout. Colouring is more of an even greyish-fawn, varying according to the area, and glands are present below the eye. There are white markings on the throat and the belly is white. The male possesses short horns.

The pigmy antelope is a sleek brown colour with a white patch beneath the throat.

Habits
Suni have similar habits to dikdik but may be more nocturnal. They are sometimes active in the early morning and late afternoon. They are primarily browsers. Suni are most often seen singly or in pairs but may be encountered in small groups. Pigmy antelope are much rarer. They are nocturnal and sometimes feed in gardens and plantations.

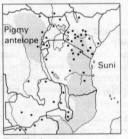

Distribution

Habitat
Suni occur in dry woodland and thornbush scrub, coastal and highland forest. The pigmy antelope is an uncommon resident of dense undergrowth at forest edges and close to cultivated areas.

Where best seen
The suni is widely spread throughout much of the region but not often identified with certainty. The pigmy antelope is confined within the region to the forest zone of western Uganda and Zaïre.

ORDER **Even toed ungulates** Artiodactyla
FAMILY **Antelopes** Bovidae

YELLOW BACKED DUIKER *Cephalophus sylvicultor*
K: Kipoke   F: Céphalophe à dos jaune   D: Riesenducker

Main colour	Shoulder height	Typical weight	Number of
Brown	85 cm, 2'10"	50 kg, 115 lb	young 1

Description
Duikers are small antelope with characteristic dark glandular markings on the face and typically a head-down, forward-sloping posture which allows them to 'dive' into the thick undergrowth they usually inhabit. Most species have a crest of hair on the crown.

The yellow backed duiker is the largest of the duiker in the region. Its general colouring is grey to dark brown with a curious yellow patch above the rump. Both sexes possess short horns which are swept backwards. There is a tuft of yellowish hair between the horns.

Habits
Relatively little is known about duikers generally on account of their habitat

and mainly nocturnal habits. This duiker is normally solitary and is rarely seen. Duiker feed on a variety of fallen fruits, leaves, seeds, fungi and, in some cases, animal matter.

Habitat
In East Africa, confined to dense highland forest.

Where best seen
Unlikely to be encountered unless deliberately sought. Occurs locally in mountain forest in western Uganda and the highlands of Kenya including the Mau escarpment.

Distribution

ORDER **Even toed ungulates** Artiodactyla
FAMILY **Antelopes** Bovidae

ABBOT'S DUIKER *Cephalophus spadix*
F: Céphalophe d'Abbot   D: Abbotducker

Main colour	Shoulder height	Typical weight	Number of young
Brown	70 cm, 2′3″	40 kg, 90 lb	1

Description
This species is a little smaller than the yellow backed duiker but very similar in general appearance. Colouring is dark brown. It does not possess the yellow dorsal patch but there may be a small greyish patch immediately above the base of the tail. Short, swept back horns are present in both sexes.

Habits
This species is mainly nocturnal and feeds primarily on fruits and berries. It inhabits high altitude forests on mountains in northern Tanzania.

Habitat
Thick montane forest.

Where best seen
Occurs on Mt Kilimanjaro b... arely seen.

Distribution

ORDER **Even toed ungulates** Artiodactyla
FAMILY **Antelopes** Bovidae

COMMON or BUSH DUIKER *Sylvicapra grimmia*
K: Nsya F: Céphalophe D: Kronenducker   Photo: page 37

 Spoor 4 cm

Main colour	Shoulder height	Typical weight	Gestation period	Number of young
Fawn	50 cm, 1'8"	16 kg, 35 lb	210 days	1

Description
Sometimes called the bush or grey duiker, this species is variously coloured fawn to grey according to the area and habitat. The male has short spiky horns. There is a black streak down the centre of the face and a short tuft of hair on the crown. The typical duiker glandular markings are present below the eyes. Common duiker have a more upright posture than other duiker and are more likely to be confused with steenbok or oribi than other duiker species.

Habits
The common duiker, although mainly nocturnal, is seen more often than other species. They emerge from cover around dusk and feed in more open areas than do other duiker species. Diet may include leaves, shoots, fruit, flowers, fungus, roots, tubers, insects and small mammals or reptiles. Common duiker seem not to need to drink. They may be solitary or in small groups.

Distribution

Habitat
Although most duiker species are confined to forest, the common duiker occurs more widely in thickish bush from coastal and riverside vegetation through suitable savanna woodlands to mountain moorlands where there is a dense cover of giant heather interspersed with grassy clearings.

Where best seen
This is the most widespread of the duikers and may be seen by chance in many areas. Very common around 10 000' on Mt Kenya and the Aberdares.

ORDER **Even toed ungulates** Artiodactyla
FAMILY **Antelopes** Bovidae

PETER'S DUIKER *Cephalophus callipygus*
F: Céphalophe de Peters   D: Petersducker

Main colour	Shoulder height	Typical weight	Number of
Reddish	50 cm, 1'8"	16 kg, 35 lb	**young** 1

Description
Several duiker species are very similar in colouring, size and shape and it can be quite confusing to identify them. This is especially so because zoological authorities do not agree on which forms constitute separate species.

Peter's is a medium sized reddish duiker, similar to the red duiker but a little larger and rather duller in colour. Coat colour varies regionally from orange to chestnut brown. The legs are grey. The similarly sized bay duiker has blacker legs and a black strip along the spine.

Habits
Peter's duiker is a diurnal species but is confined to true forest. They seem to feed mainly on fallen flowers, fruit and fungus from the forest floor. They are preyed upon by leopard and golden cat.

Habitat
Peter's duiker is associated with true forest in the Central African block. It also occurs in Uganda and in suitable highland forest also in Kenya.

Where best seen
Within the forest zone of Zaïre and western Uganda. Peter's duiker occurs in Kenya on Mt Elgon and the Mau escarpment.

Distribution

ORDER **Even toed ungulates** Artiodactyla
FAMILY **Antelopes** Bovidae

BLACK FRONTED DUIKER *Cephalophus nigrifrons*
K: Kichachu

Spoor
4 cm

Main colour	Shoulder height	Typical weight	Number of
Russet	50 cm, 1'8"	14 kg, 30 lb	young 1

Description
The black fronted duiker is a little longer limbed than the similar red duiker and is darker in colour, a reddish-brown which varies regionally. The front of the face is black, as is the crest of hair between the horns. The lower parts of the legs are darker than the rest of the body.

Habits
This is a higher altitude species than the red duiker, occurring generally above 8000' in the eastern part of the region. It is mainly nocturnal but is sometimes seen during the day especially in dull weather. Diet consists of a wide variety of fruit and vegetable matter.

Distribution

Habitat
The black fronted duiker occurs in high altitude forest and mountain moorland, in generally moister localities than the red duiker. It occurs in lowland swamp forest further west.

Where best seen
Black fronted duiker may be seen in suitable habitat above 8000' in the Volcanoes, Ruwenzoris and Mts Elgon and Kenya.

ORDER **Even toed ungulates** Artiodactyla
FAMILY **Antelopes** Bovidae

WHITE BELLIED DUIKER *Cephalophus leucogaster*
BAY DUIKER *Cephalophus dorsalis*

F: Céphalophe à ventre blanc, Céphalophe bai D: Weissbauchducker, Schwarzruckenducker

White bellied duiker

Bay duiker

Main colour	Shoulder height	Typical weight	Number of young
Russet	40 cm, 1'4"	14 kg, 30 lb	1

Description
The white bellied duiker has a characteristic white underside and is a generally paler colour than the similar black fronted duiker. There is a greyish or black strip along the spine and the face is black. The crest is orange in colour.

The bay duiker is another medium-sized species, slightly heavier in build but of generally similar russet colouring to several other species. The legs are noticeably darker in colour and there is a black band along the spine which is rather more prominent than in the white bellied duiker.

Distribution

Habits
The white bellied duiker is mainly diurnal and feeds on fruits and leaves. The bay duiker is nocturnal and appears to have a higher proportion of animal matter in its diet. It is rather rare and thinly spread.

Habitat
Both of these species are associated with dense lowland forest in central Africa.

Where best seen
Relatively uncommon species confined to true forest in Zaïre.

ORDER **Even toed ungulates** Artiodactyla
FAMILY **Antelopes** Bovidae

RED DUIKER *Cephalophus harveyi*
RUWENZORI RED DUIKER *Cephalophus rubidus*
NATAL RED DUIKER *Cephalophus natalensis*

K: Funo F: Céphalophe rouge D: Rotducker

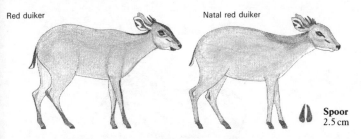

Spoor
2.5 cm

Main colour	Shoulder height	Typical weight	Number of young
Russet	40 cm, 1′4″	12 kg, 26 lb	1

Description
There is a great deal of variability within, and similarity between, certain duiker species. This is typified by the red duikers, which are themselves similar to others already described.

The red duiker has a bright orange-brown coat and both sexes possess short straight horns. The typical duiker facial glands and tufty crest are present. There is often a dark front to the face which can cause some confusion with the black fronted duiker.

The closely allied Natal red duiker does not have a black face. This species occurs in southern Tanzania and further south. The Ruwenzori red duiker has a pale belly and is confined to the alpine zones on the Ruwenzori Mountains.

Habits
Red duiker have been little studied on account of their habitat and retiring nature. They occur in pairs, or alone, and although mainly nocturnal, may occasionally be seen during daylight hours. They eat fallen fruit and berries and they use a communal dung heap.

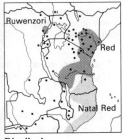

Habitat
Dense coastal and riverine forest, highland forests with dense secondary growth.

Where best seen
Red duiker are widespread in the eastern part of the region but in discontinuous localities. Often seen below 8000′ in the Aberdares salient. Also occur on the Tana and Voi rivers in eastern Kenya.

Distribution

ORDER **Even toed ungulates** Artiodactyla
FAMILY **Antelopes** Bovidae

RED FLANKED DUIKER *Cephalophus rufilatus*
K: Funo F: Céphalophe à flancs roux D: Rotflankenducker

Main colour	Shoulder height	Typical weight	Number of
Orange	40 cm, 1'4"	10 kg, 22 lb	young 1

Description
This is one of the smaller duiker species, generally rather similar to the red duikers. Its colouring is a brighter orange, especially on the flanks. The face is black and the lower parts of the legs are grey. The back is greyish but quite variable from area to area.

Distribution

Habits
The red flanked duiker is active mostly in early mornings and evenings and feeds in more open locations than many other duikers.

Habitat
This is a species of the forest edge, occurring in areas of thick grass and scrub rather than true forest.

Where best seen
Not uncommon within its habitat but occurs only marginally within the East African region.

ORDER **Even toed ungulates** Artiodactyla
FAMILY **Antelopes** Bovidae

ZANZIBAR or ADER'S DUIKER *Cephalophus adersi*
K: Nunga   F: Céphalophe d'Ader   D: Aderducker

Main colour	Shoulder height	Typical weight	Number of
Russet	35 cm, 1'2"	5 kg, 11 lb	**young** 1

Description
A very small orange-tan duiker with a characteristic white band across the flanks. There are white spots on the legs. Both sexes have short horns and the typical duiker facial glands and crest are present. Also referred to as dwarf red duiker.

Distribution

Habits
A very secretive and rare duiker about which little is known. Mainly nocturnal, solitary or occurring in pairs.

Habitat
Dense coastal bush and forest.

Where best seen
Occurs in a number of coastal locations in Kenya and Tanzania as well as the islands of Zanzibar and Pemba. It is rarely seen and must be considered threatened on account of the destruction of its forest habitat.

ORDER **Even toed ungulates** Artiodactyla
FAMILY **Antelopes** Bovidae

BLUE DUIKER *Cephalophus monticola*
K: Paa, ndimba   F: Céphalophe bleu   D: Blauducker

Spoor
2 cm

Main colour	Shoulder height	Typical weight	Gestation period	Number of
Grey	30 cm, 1'	4 kg, 9 lb	115 days	**young** 1

Description
The blue duiker is one of the smallest duikers. It gives more an impression of a scurrying rabbit than anything else. It is variously coloured in shades of grey or brown according to region and some individuals have a bluish tinge in certain lights. As with many duikers, the rump is rounded and set higher than the neck. Tiny horns are usually present in the male but absent from specimens in some areas. The usual duiker glands are present. It has a white tail.

Habits
Little is known about this species as it is rarely encountered, although reputedly not uncommon within the dense undergrowth of its habitat. Leaves, seeds and fruits form much of its diet. This species is mainly active around dusk and dawn.

Habitat
Dense coastal or riverine forest, highland forests, scrub and thick bush.

Where best seen
Difficult to see anywhere although widespread in suitable localities and not uncommon.

Distribution

ORDER **Even toed ungulates** Artiodactyla
FAMILY **Pigs** Suidae

GIANT FOREST HOG *Hylochoerus meinertzhageni*
K: Nguruwe   F: Hylochère géant   D: Waldschwein

Main colour	Shoulder height	Typical weight	Gestation period
Black	82 cm, 2'8"	135 kg, 300 lb	130 days

Description
A very large, heavily built pig, black in colour and covered with coarse hair. Large swellings are present beneath the eye and these are especially marked in older males. Males also possess tusks which curve outward from the snout. The general appearance is very pig-like but much bigger than the warthog.

Habits
Giant forest hog occur often in family groups of up to 8 animals. They are mainly nocturnal but forage throughout the day in some localities. Although generally confined to a concealing habitat, they do emerge into open clearings to feed.

Distribution

Habitat
This species is associated with dense undergrowth in forested areas. It seems especially fond of forests with open grassy clearings interspersed with thick bush. In East Africa, it is confined to riverine and montane forests between 6000' and 8000'.

Where best seen
Occurs in riverine forests in Serengeti and Mara and in the highland forest of the Ruwenzoris, Mt Elgon, Mt Kenya and the Aberdares. It can easily be seen in the Aberdares salient.

ORDER **Even toed ungulates** Artiodactyla
FAMILY **Pigs** Suidae

WARTHOG *Phacochoerus aethiopicus*
K: Ngiri   F: Phacochère   D: Warzenschwein

Photo: page 45

Spoor
5 cm

Main colour	Shoulder height	Typical weight	Gestation period	Number of young
Grey brown	65 cm, 2'2"	75 kg, 165 lb	170 days	1–8

Description
A charcoal grey to tawny coated pig with a heavily warted face and a solid, compact appearance. There is a sparse covering of bristly hairs on the body and a slight ridge down the spine. Tusks are present which curve boldly up from the snout. Smaller, blade-like tusks emerge horizontally from the lower jaw. For a small animal, warthog can be surprisingly heavy at up to 100 kg.

Habits
Warthog may be seen during daylight hours in small family groups rooting in the earth for rhizomes. They also feed on grass by kneeling down on their front legs. Litters of up to 8 young may accompany the adults. Warthog live in burrows and they enjoy wallowing in mud, which colours their body according to the colour of the local earth. They have an amusing habit of running off with tails held stiffly vertical like radio aerials.

Habitat
Savanna, open and lightly wooded country, especially near lakes and waterways. Although often associated with wet and muddy places, warthog also occur in quite dry areas where water may only occasionally be available.

Where best seen
Reasonably common throughout their range and seen in most of the savanna, forest and highland parks of the region.

Distribution

ORDER **Even toed ungulates** Artiodactyla
FAMILY **Pigs** Suidae

BUSHPIG *Potamochoerus porcus*
K: Nguruwe   F: Potamochère   D: Buschschwein

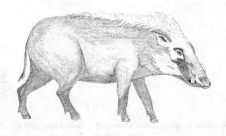

Spoor
5 cm

Main colour	Shoulder height	Typical weight	Gestation period	Number of
Russet	70 cm, 2'4"	70 kg, 155 lb	120 days	young 1−8

Description
A reddish to brownish pig with white or yellow bristles along the face and neck. More hairy overall than the warthog and lacks the facial warts. Small tusks may be present.

Habits
Bushpigs are primarily nocturnal but otherwise share similar habits with the warthog. They wallow in mud, live in well-concealed earths and feed on almost anything, including roots, fruits, insects and carrion. Reputed to be quite common as they can be difficult to eradicate from farms and agricultural areas. Nevertheless, rarely seen.

Habitat
Associated with moist areas with plenty of dense cover. Forest and thick bush close to water seem to be the preferred habitat.

Where best seen
Not often encountered on safari on account of their nocturnal habits and the cover afforded by the habitat. May be seen after dark rooting around some camps and lodges, especially in highland areas.

Distribution

ORDER **Even toed ungulates** Artiodactyla
FAMILY **Hippopotamus** Hippopotamidae

HIPPOPOTAMUS *Hippopotamus amphibius*
K: Kiboko   F: Hippopotame   D: Grossflusspferd   **Photo:** page 45

Spoor
20 cm

Main colour	Shoulder height	Typical weight	Gestation period	Number of young
Grey	1.5 m, 5′	1500 kg, 3300 lb	240 days	1

Description
A bulky, grey and pink, piggy-eyed animal nearly always found in or close to water. Nostrils and eyes are bulbous so that they may emerge from the water without revealing the bulk that lies beneath. Hippo possess long incisor teeth that may be visible when feeding or yawning. These tusks can measure 25 cm. The spoor of the hippo shows four toes compared with the rhino's three.

Habits
Hippo lie up in waterways during the day, emerging at night to graze on grass. They also feed on various floating plants. They are often found in groups, up to several dozen, in the water, but are otherwise solitary. Individuals are sometimes encountered during the day well away from water and they may roam very large distances across dry country as pools dry up after the rains. Beaten muddy pathways show where hippo leave the water each night. Their gruff snorting may be heard at all hours.

Habitat
Rivers, lakes, swamps with permanent water. Adjacent grassland is required for feeding and close-cropped lawns can result. Hippo are somewhat depleted from their former range but still common in many areas.

Where best seen
Many lakes and rivers throughout the region, especially in protected areas. Most numerous in Virunga and Ruwenzori, also Lake Malaŵi and the Luangwa and Kafue Rivers.

Distribution

| ORDER | **Even toed ungulates** Artiodactyla |
| FAMILY | **Giraffes** Giraffidae |

GIRAFFE *Giraffa camelopardalis*
K: Twiga F: Giraffe D: Giraffe

Masai giraffe

Southern giraffe

Spoor 20 cm

Main colour	Overall height	Typical weight	Gestation period	Number of young
Russet	5 m, 16 ft	1000 kg, 2200 lb	15 months	1

Description
Giraffe are the tallest mammals in the world. There are several races of giraffe with the common or Masai giraffe of the region possessing typical jagged markings in shades of reddish brown. This race has two short horns while others may have three or even five. Colouring varies regionally, between races, and individually. Older bulls tend to be darker, sometimes very dark brown. The lower part of the legs is usually patterned in the Masai race. Giraffe in the southern part of the region are generally paler in colour with less jagged markings. Thornicroft's giraffe is much darker in colour and is confined to the Luangwa valley.

Habits
Giraffe have a very loose social structure and may be encountered singly, in small groups or in herds of 20 or more. Females and young gather in small nursery herds. They are not dependent on water but will drink if it is available although they are shy, since their splay-legged posture renders them vulnerable to lion attack. Giraffe may wait long periods to be sure that predators are not present before drinking. Males spar for dominance in prolonged bouts of 'necking' in which each in turn swings its neck forcibly against the other's.

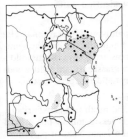

Habitat
A browser generally found in open woodlands and lightly wooded savanna as well as immediately adjacent grasslands. Giraffe consume thorny acacia branches often leaving trees cropped in an hourglass shape along the line of browsing.

Where best seen
In most of the savanna reserves of the southern Kenya, Tanzania and Zambia.

Distribution

ORDER **Even toed ungulates** Artiodactyla
FAMILY **Giraffes** Giraffidae

RETICULATED GIRAFFE *Giraffa camelopardalis reticulata*
K: Twiga   F: Giraffe   D: Giraffe

Photo: page 38

Reticulated giraffe

Rothschild's giraffe

Spoor
18 cm

Main colour	Overall height	Typical weight	Gestation period	Number of young
Chestnut	4.5 m, 14'8"	950 kg, 2100 lb	15 months	1

Description
Giraffe are nowadays considered to belong to a single species but the reticulated giraffe is sufficiently different to merit separate description. It is a three-horned giraffe with starkly delineated polygonal markings in rich russet colouring. Markings continue well down the legs. It is not quite so large as the Masai race. A further race, Rothschild's giraffe, possess apparently hybrid features. It is paler than the reticulated but with similar if less dramatic markings. It may have three or five horns and the lower legs are white.

Habits
Similar to the common or Masai giraffe. The reticulated giraffe inhabits arid areas and is less dependent on water.

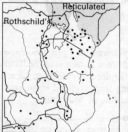
Distribution

Habitat
Dry thornbush and lightly wooded savanna. The reticulated giraffe is found throughout the semi-desert scrub of north eastern Kenya. Rothschild's giraffe occurs in open grasslands and light woodland in western Kenya and northern Uganda.

Where best seen
Samburu and Meru and north to Lake Turkana. Rothschild's giraffe is less common but a herd has been relocated into Lake Nakuru park.

ORDER **Even toed ungulates** Artiodactyla
FAMILY **Giraffes** Giraffidae

OKAPI *Okapia johnstoni*
K: Okapi F: Okapi D: Okapi

Main colour	Shoulder height	Typical weight	Gestation period	Number of young
Reddish	1.7 m, 5'6"	250 kg, 550 lb	14 months	1

Description
Although related to the giraffes, the okapi has a much shorter neck. Its overall shape is otherwise quite similar. It is a wine red in colour, with a pattern of horizontal white stripes on the legs and the hindquarters. The lower parts of the legs are white. Bony knobs grow on the crown rather like giraffes' horns.

Habits
Generally solitary or in pairs, okapi feed on leaves and twigs deep inside dense forest.

Habitat
Confined to true rain forest in eastern and central Zaïre.

Where best seen
Rarely seen in the wild but can be viewed at the capture station at Epulu in eastern Zaïre.

Distribution

ORDER **Odd toed ungulates** Perissodactyla
FAMILY **Zebras** Equidae

GREVY'S ZEBRA *Equus grevyi*
F: Zèbre de Grévy D: Grevyzebra

Photo: pages 38, 46

Spoor
15 cm

Main colour	Shoulder height	Typical weight	Gestation period	Number of young
Black and white	1.50 m, 5'	350 kg, 770 lb	390 days	1

Description
The largest of the zebra species, Grevy's has narrow stripes over the body, rump and legs. The stripes are broader on the neck. The belly is white. On the rump, the stripes fall into a fine circular pattern which is characteristic. Other distinguishing features are the tufty ears and a coarse mane.

Habits
Unlike the common zebra, herds of Grevy's accumulate during the wet season, spreading out more thinly in the dry times in order better to exploit the meagre food resources of their arid habitat. Herds are not large, typically 8–30, though this may reflect the rarity of the species. They are grazers. Mixed groups of common and Grevy's zebra occur from time to time in the narrow zone where they overlap.

Habitat
Confined to the dry semi-desert and thornbush savanna of northern Kenya (and southern Ethiopia).

Where best seen
Samburu and Meru. Also occurs in significant numbers on ranches in Kenya's Laikipia district. The centre of concentration lies east of Lake Turkana and includes Sibiloi.

Distribution

ORDER **Odd toed ungulates** Perissodactyla
FAMILY **Zebras** Equidae

COMMON or BURCHELL'S ZEBRA *Equus burchelli*
K: Punda milia F: Zèbre de steppe D: Steppenzebra

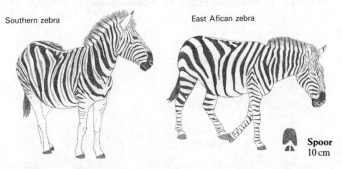

Southern zebra   East Afican zebra

Spoor
10 cm

Main colour	Shoulder height	Typical weight	Gestation period	Number of young
Black and white	1.3 m, 4'3"	310 kg, 680 lb	375 days	1

Description
The 'striped donkey' of the African savanna. The East African race has broad, well-defined stripes over the entire body and legs down to the knees. From southern Tanzania southwards, zebra are found with more or less clear brown 'shadow' stripes between the black ones. Zebras' stripes are quite variable in intensity and the patterning is also variable to the extent that it may be possible to recognise individual animals from their markings.

Habits
A gregarious creature occurring in herds that may be thousands strong during dry season concentrations and migrations. Zebra rely on regular access to water and develop daily routines, drinking in the early morning and trekking, often long distances, into the bush during the day. They spread widely, and more thinly, over the savanna when the rains produce a flush of green grass. Common zebra migrate with other plains species such as wildebeest. Males fight on their hind legs before the breeding season and emit a characteristic repetitive whinnying cry.

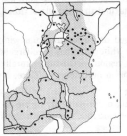

Habitat
Open grassland and light woodland with access to water. Zebra always seem to look fat, sleek and healthy but their dependency on water and grazing renders them vulnerable to drought, especially where migration routes are blocked.

Where best seen
Grassy plains throughout the region. Dry season concentrations in Amboseli, Mara and Serengeti.

Distribution

ORDER **Odd toed ungulates** Perissodactyla
FAMILY **Rhinoceroses** Rhinocerotidae

WHITE or SQUARE-LIPPED RHINOCEROS
Ceratotherium simum
K: Kifaru   F: Rhinocéros blanc   D: Breitmaulnashorn

Spoor
22 cm

Main colour	Shoulder height	Typical weight	Gestation period	Number of
Grey brown	1.8 m, 5'10"	2000 kg, 4400 lb	16 months	**young** 1

Description
A large, prehistoric looking creature with a heavily creased brown to grey skin and two horns on the nose. The white rhino is the larger of the two African rhino species, weighing up to 2 tonnes. It has a square face adapted to grazing. The black rhino possesses a hooked top lip. The horns, formed by compacted hair, are very variable in size. The spoor is like that of the hippo but with only three toes.

Habits
Diurnal where protected but often nocturnal. White rhino are more gregarious than the black and gather in small groups — where there are enough of them left to do so. Rhino have poor eyesight but good hearing and sense of smell. White rhino tend to be more placid and less notoriously temperamental than the black rhino.

Distribution

Habitat
Rhino require wooded or bushy grassland with access to water. The white rhino has been largely poached out of the region, occurring naturally now only in Garamba in north eastern Zaïre.

Where best seen
White rhino now only occur naturally in the region in Garamba. They are much more numerous in parts of southern Africa.

ORDER **Odd toed ungulates** Perissodactyla
FAMILY **Rhinoceroses** Rhinocerotidae

BLACK or HOOK-LIPPED RHINOCEROS
Diceros bicornis
K: Kifaru   F: Rhinocéros noir   D: Spitzmaulnashorn   **Photo:** pages 39, 46

See page 132

Spoor
20 cm

Main colour	Shoulder height	Typical weight	Gestation period	Number of
Grey brown	1.6 m, 5'3"	1000 kg, 2200 lb	15 months	**young** 1

Description
Slightly smaller and rather less bulky than the white rhino but nevertheless a large creature. The black rhino is a browser and possesses a hooked top lip to help gather twigs and shoots. The silhouette of rhinos shows two humps, one at the shoulder and the other at the rump. The two horns are very variable in size, the front horn usually but not always being the longer. The spoor is like that of the hippo but with only three toes.

Habits
Diurnal where protected but often strictly nocturnal. Black rhino tend to be solitary while white rhino are more gregarious but small groups of two or three are sometimes encountered. Young stay with the mother until quite well grown. Their eyesight is very poor and they may be quite unaware of an intruder until it is very close. When disturbed, a black rhino will either charge or flee with its tail in the air until it vanishes over the horizon. They will charge vehicles if they approach within a certain critical distance. Lion sometimes prey on young rhino.

Habitat
Both rhino species require wooded or bushy grassland with access to water. Black rhino may be found in highland forest areas as well as in thick scrub at the edges of savanna.

Distribution

Where best seen
Rhino have suffered severely from poaching throughout the region and are far less common than just a few years ago. Black rhino can be seen in Mara and Amboseli, but they are few, and in Nairobi where they have been translocated. More numerous in the Aberdares where they are nocturnal. Sanctuaries have been established in certain Kenyan parks and on private land. Still fairly numerous in Luangwa valley.

Black or hook-lipped rhinoceros

African elephant

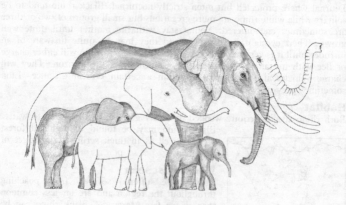

Adult ♂
Adult ♀
15 years
6 years   2 years   1 year

ORDER **Proboscidea**
FAMILY **Elephants** Elephantidae

AFRICAN ELEPHANT *Loxodanta africana*
K: Ndovu, tembo   F: Eléphant   D: Grosselefant   Photo: 39, 40, 47

See page 132

Spoor
50 cm

Main colour	Shoulder height	Typical weight	Gestation period	Number of
Grey	3 m, 10'	5500 kg, 12000 lb	22 months	**young** 1

Description
At six tonnes, the African elephant is quite the bulkiest land mammal. It differs from the Indian elephant in having larger ears and tusks. Both sexes grow tusks, those of the male being larger, but sizes vary considerably from area to area. Males are generally heavier and more solitary than the females. They have a more rounded forehead compared with the angular front of the female's head. The forest elephant of central and west Africa is rather smaller with more slender tusks. It is recognised as a separate subspecies from the savanna elephant.

Habits
Herds generally consist of females and young with males present only for breeding. Males may be solitary or in small groups. Elephant often follow a daily routine, moving between feeding grounds and water where they often bathe and drink during the hotter hours. They are active by day and night as their bulk demands a continual intake of food, up to 300 kg or 660 lb a day. Elephant present a formidable sight when they raise their ears at an intruder but it is not possible to predict with certainty if they will charge. Individual temperament seems to be a key factor. Elephant have a wide repertoire of grunts, squeals, rumbles and snorts as well as their blood-curdling trumpeting.

Habitat
Adapted to a wide variety of habitats including forest, woodland, mountains and semi-desert, from sea level to 10 000', but dependent on woodland for feeding. They migrate in some areas but scope for this has been largely reduced.

Distribution

Where best seen
Recent surveys show that 60–70% of elephant throughout East Africa were eliminated, mainly through poaching, between 1977 and 1987. The rate of decline will make them an endangered species very soon. Poaching continues, but sizeable elephant herds may still be seen in Amboseli, Lake Manyara, Selous, Luangwa and a few other parks of the region.

ORDER **Carnivores** Carnivora
FAMILY **Hyenas** Hyaenidae

SPOTTED HYENA *Crocuta crocuta*
K: Fisi F: Hyène tachetée D: Fleckenhyäne

Photo: page 47

Spoor
10 cm

Main colour	Shoulder height	Typical weight	Gestation period	Number of
Fawn	80 cm, 2'7"	65 kg, 145 lb	110 days	young 1–4

Description
A large, dog-like animal with prominent ears, a sloping back, spotted golden coat and a loping gait. Hyenas often have a dishevelled appearance on account of their muddy and bloody habits. The eerie whooping sound made by the spotted hyena at night is one of the most evocative sounds of the African bush. Groups around a kill may indulge in a series of spine-chilling cackles and whoops. Spotted hyena are the most common of the hyenas but may be one of the first animals to disappear in the face of human settlement.

Habits
Mainly nocturnal but often seen during the day. Although reputed to be cowardly, and indeed their hesitant but persistent method of attack gives all the appearance of cowardice, hyenas often actively hunt. They scavenge as well, of course, and may be encountered on safari at the site of a kill where they do battle with their own kind, with lion or even vultures for a share of the pickings. Hyenas live in dens excavated in muddy banks or anthills.

Habitat
Open savanna, lightly wooded areas and semi-desert. They require regular access to water but as with many mammals, seem to be able to survive long periods without drinking.

Where best seen
Common throughout the region and often spotted where carcasses can be located by following the descent of vultures. Often seen emerging from cover before dusk.

Distribution

ORDER **Carnivores** Carnivora
FAMILY **Hyenas** Hyaenidae

STRIPED HYENA *Hyaena hyaena*
K: Fisi   F: Hyène rayée   D: Streifenhyäne   **Photo:** page 48

Main colour	Shoulder height	Gestation period	Number of
Grey	75 cm, 2'6"	95 days	young 2–4

Description
A shaggy, dog-like animal, lighter in build than the spotted hyena. It is generally grey or brownish in colour with a pattern of vertical black stripes. The ears are pointed and there is a dorsal crest of hair which leads along the back to a pale bushy tail.

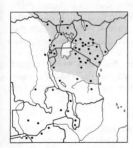

Distribution

Habits
The striped hyena is more strictly nocturnal than the spotted and rather less common. It is much more timid and generally solitary.

Habitat
Occurs in a variety of habitats but most often associated with rocky and broken hilly terrain with a fair amount of bush cover.

Where best seen
Rarely encountered on account of its nocturnal nature and retiring habits.

ORDER **Carnivores** Carnivora
FAMILY **Hyenas** Hyaenidae

AARDWOLF *Proteles cristeles*
K: Fisi ndogo   F: Protèle   D: Erdwolf

Spoor
4.5 cm

Main colour	Shoulder height	Typical weight	Gestation period	Number of
Grey brown	50 cm, 1'8"	9 kg, 20 lb	60 days	young 2–4

Description
A rather dainty, dog-like creature with a very bushy tail and a furry dorsal mane. Overall colouring is sandy brown with distinctive and fairly constant stripe patterning. Although related to the hyenas, the aardwolf has diminutive molar teeth adapted to its specialised diet.

Habits
The aardwolf is mainly nocturnal and normally quite solitary. Principal food consists of certain species of termites which are 'grazed' up from the ground in a manner apparently quite unsuited to this sort of creature. In fact, the insects are lapped up with the particularly long tongue, which has a special coating of scales and sticky saliva for the purpose. When alarmed, the aardwolf raises its mane and appears almost to double in size.

Habitat
Generally associated with savanna and semi-desert areas where their preferred food supply of termites inhabit underground chambers from which they emerge at night. This is often on firm sandy soils which support a growth of thornbush. They are independent of water. Although widely spread, aardwolf are considered rare but, as with many nocturnal animals, may be more common than thought.

Where best seen
May be encountered at night or in the very early mornings anywhere within their range. Tsavo East is typical of suitable habitat.

Distribution

ORDER **Carnivores** Carnivora
FAMILY **Dogs, jackals and foxes** Canidae

WILD or HUNTING DOG *Lycaon pictus*
K: Mbwa mwitu   F: Cynhyène   D: Hyänenhund

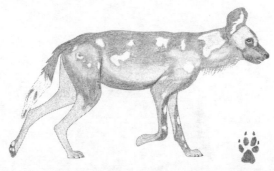

Spoor
8 cm

Main colour	Shoulder height	Typical weight	Gestation period	Number of
Fawn and black	70 cm, 2'3"	20 kg, 44 lb	70 days	young 2–19

Description
A very dog-like animal with a distinctively blotched coat in shades of white, fawn and black. They have bushy tails with white tips and huge saucer-shaped ears. The alternative name of hunting dog still persists but has given rise to a largely undeserved reputation for evil.

Habits
Wild dogs are particularly adapted to living in packs of up to 15 or more. They hunt collectively by running prey to exhaustion while snapping at its heels. This has given them a rather bloodthirsty name but once food is available, the young are allowed to eat first. They hunt during the day but sometimes at night as well. They utter a kind of chirruping noise in addition to a variety of other more dog-like sounds.

Distribution

Habitat
Often in open plains where their eyesight can be utilised to locate prey but also in some wooded areas. They are not normally found in forest or dense bush but may lie up in thornbush or rocky areas.

Where best seen
Wild dogs have been exterminated in many areas and seem to have suffered from disease in others. They may now be considered rare in much of the region and are not often seen. They do occur in Mara and Serengeti, amongst other places.

ORDER **Carnivores** Carnivora
FAMILY **Dogs, jackals and foxes** Canidae

BLACK BACKED JACKAL *Canis mesomelas*
K: Bweha   F: Chacal à chabraque   D: Schabrackenschakal   **Photo:** page 48

Spoor
4 cm

Main colour	Shoulder height	Typical weight	Gestation period	Number of young
Russet and black	40 cm, 1'4"	8 kg, 18 lb	60 days	1–6

Description
A dog-shaped animal with an ochreous orange colour on its flanks and neck and a pronounced black or silvery grey saddle. Its tail is tipped black. Ears are upright and alert in appearance. The black backed jackal has a trotting gait.

Habits
The black backed jackal exhibits both nocturnal and diurnal activity. It is a solitary creature and has an omnivorous diet consisting of insects, small birds and mammals and carrion taken from larger predators' kills. It sometimes opportunistically follows predators such as cheetah while they are hunting. These jackals have a characteristic yelping noise which can be heard at night and a howling chorus occasionally heard at sunset.

Habitat
A wide variety of savanna and semi-desert habitats.

Where best seen
Common throughout the region.

Distribution

ORDER **Carnivores** Carnivora
FAMILY **Dogs, jackals and foxes** Canidae

SIDE STRIPED JACKAL *Canis adustus*
K: Bweha   F: Chacal à flancs rayés   D: Streifenschakal

Spoor
4 cm

Main colour	Shoulder height	Typical weight	Gestation period	Number of
Grey	40 cm, 1'4"	9 kg, 20 lb	60 days	young 4–6

Description
Very similar in size and shape to the black backed jackal. The side striped jackal is grey in colour, sometimes with a yellowish hue. It has a pale stripe diagonally along the side of the body and the tail is tipped white.

Habits
The side striped jackal is more strictly nocturnal than the black backed but is occasionally seen during the day. Also solitary, or in pairs, it has a similar diet that may include fruit and vegetable matter. These jackals have a melancholy repetitive yelp.

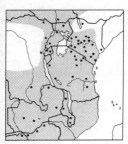

Habitat
The side striped jackal prefers moister, more wooded areas than the black backed.

Where best seen
Although just as widely spread as the black backed jackal, the side striped is less often seen, probably on account of its nocturnal habits. It seems to be more common in the south of the region.

Distribution

ORDER **Carnivores** Carnivora
FAMILY **Dogs, jackals and foxes** Canidae

GOLDEN JACKAL *Canis aureus*
K: Bweha   F: Chacal doré   D: Goldschakal

Spoor
4 cm

Main colour	Shoulder height	Typical weight	Gestation period	Number of young
Fawn	40 cm, 1'4"	8 kg, 18 lb	60 days	3–8

Description
A pale sandy or yellowish jackal of much the same size and shape as the other two species. There is a fair degree of variability in colouring and it is easy to confuse the golden jackal with the side striped in some areas where there may be some interbreeding. Elsewhere, it is clearly a yellower colour. The tip of the tail is usually dark.

Habits
Nocturnal but also partly diurnal. Usually solitary but sometimes in pairs. Golden jackal have been observed rearing young in earths dug into the ground.

Habitat
Bush and grass savanna. More associated with plains than the other species but overlapping in distribution.

Where best seen
Sometimes encountered during the day in Serengeti and Ngorongoro.

Distribution

ORDER **Carnivores** Carnivora
FAMILY **Dogs, jackals and foxes** Canidae

BAT EARED FOX *Otocyon megalotis*
F: Otocyon   D: Löffelhund

Photo: page 49

Spoor
4 cm

Main colour	Shoulder height	Typical weight	Gestation period	Number of young 4–6
Grey	30 cm, 1'	4 kg, 9 lb	65 days	

Description
A small fox with a bushy black tail and enormous ears in relation to its size. Overall colour is fawny grey fading into a yellower tone on the face. The muzzle and cheeks are black, contrasting sharply with the sides of the mouth and a band across the brow which are much paler.

Habits
The huge ears of these foxes are used to locate the movements of insects, beetle larvae, scorpions and small mammals amongst the grass roots and just below the ground. The ears are held closely parallel to the ground and the prey is quickly excavated by the powerful forefeet. Bat eared foxes inhabit dens dug into the earth. They may be active during the day or at night and are often seen scampering across the plains to the cover of their dens.

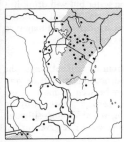

Habitat
Open grassy plains in the savanna areas of the region.

Where best seen
Flat, open, shortgrass plains throughout their range, typically Mara and Serengeti.

Distribution

ORDER **Carnivores** Carnivora
FAMILY **Cats** Felidae

LION *Panthera leo*
K: Simba   F: Lion   D: Löwe

Spoor
12 cm

	♀	♂		
Main colour	**Shoulder height**	**Typical weight**	**Gestation period**	**Number of**
Fawn	1 m, 3'4"	200 kg, 440 lb	110 days	**young** 1–6

Description
The largest of the African cats, generally a golden sandy colour except for the male's mane which may be darker or even black. Lion from some areas are greyer in colour. Undersides are paler and juveniles retain spotting on the bellies and sides until quite well grown. Females are maneless but maneless males are also found.

Habits
The so-called 'king of the jungle' sleeps for two thirds of the day and is rarely found in real jungle. Normally spending the hotter hours of the day in deep shade, lion go on the prowl as night falls, emitting a series of deep descending grunts that carries for long distances. Lion hunt actively every three or four days, usually in the very early morning. Prides of females and young may number up to 20, though such large prides are becoming rare. Males are more solitary and roam alone or in pairs. In some areas, lion scavenge from hyena kills, which is opposite to what is normally supposed.

Habitat
Lion can occur in most habitats but it is unusual to find them in true forest.

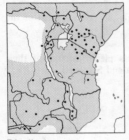

Distribution

They do not depend on water but will drink if it is available. Prides occupy well defined territories but lone males are great wanderers and may turn up in a variety of areas and habitats.

Where best seen
Very much depleted from its original range, the lion may be considered uncommon outside protected areas. They can be seen in most of the parks of the region, perhaps most easily in Amboseli, Mara, Serengeti and Virunga although also often seen in the more wooded reserves further south.

ORDER **Carnivores** Carnivora
FAMILY **Cats** Felidae

LEOPARD *Panthera pardus*
K: Chui   F: Panthère   D: Leopard

Spoor
8 cm

Main colour	Shoulder height	Typical weight	Gestation period	Number of
Fawn	65 cm, 2'2"	Male: 60 kg, 130 lb Female: 35 kg, 75 lb	100 days	young 1–6

Description
One of the larger cats, with a distinctive rosette patterned coat. The leopard has a 'low-slung' appearance compared with lion or cheetah. Colour is variable with ground colour ranging from the usual golden tawny through dusky grey to almost pure black in some individuals. Even on darker specimens, the pattern of rosettes can be made out.

Habits
A stealthy, nocturnal creature only occasionally seen during daylight. May spend part of the day in caves or rocky areas or lying along the branch of a tree in savanna or forested areas. Feeds on a wide variety of prey, from hyrax and baboons to antelope and zebra. Leopard possess amazing strength and are able to carry prey such as antelope or zebra into the branches of a tree away from the reach of hyenas and vultures.

Distribution

Habitat
Rocky gorges, wooded watercourses, forest, almost any broken country where there is cover and prey. Normally require access to water. Less rare than often thought, due to its secretive habits, the leopard still occurs close to urban centres in many parts of Africa and is regularly seen on the outskirts of Nairobi.

Where best seen
Widely but thinly spread throughout the region. May be chanced upon in most parks. Nowadays attracted by bait to some tourist lodges. Black specimens occur in highland areas such as the Aberdares.

ORDER **Carnivores** Carnivora
FAMILY **Cats** Felidae

CHEETAH *Acinonyx jubatus*
K: Duma F: Guepard D: Gepard   Photo: Page 40

Spoor
9 cm

Main colour	Shoulder height	Typical weight	Gestation period	Number of
Fawn	80 cm, 2′7″	60 kg, 130 lb	90 days	young 1–5

Description
A large cat, of similar shoulder height to but much more slimly built than the leopard. A small head, lithe appearance and spotted coat are distinctive. The spots are not arranged in any particular pattern but may tend to follow the spine on the back. Black 'teardrop' markings are visible on the face. Young cheetah possess a raised mane on the neck until about 18 months old. The cheetah is not considered a true cat as its claws have no protective sheaths and remain exposed even when retracted.

Habits
Cheetah are diurnal hunters, normally associated with open plains where their famed high speed hunting abilities can be utilised. They cannot maintain a chase for more than a few seconds, however. They prey upon birds such as francolin and bustard as well as small mammals like gazelle. Cheetah have a nervous disposition and are easily chased off prey by hyenas, lions or humans. This may be one reason why cheetah have declined throughout most of their range. Cheetah may be encountered singly, in pairs or in small family groups with up to 4 young, which are reared by the female.

Distribution

Habitat
Although grassy savanna and lightly wooded plains are classic cheetah country, they are also found in areas of thornbush scrub and semi-desert.

Where best seen
Thinly spread but often seen in Nairobi, Amboseli, Mara, Samburu and Serengeti.

ORDER **Carnivores** Carnivora
FAMILY **Cats** Felidae

SERVAL *Felis serval*
K: Mondo F: Serval D: Servalkatze

Photo: page 50

Spoor
3.5 cm

Main colour	Shoulder height	Typical weight	Gestation period	Number of
Fawn	55 cm, 1'10"	12 kg, 26 lb	70 days	young 1–3

Description
A small spotted cat with prominent ears, a short ringed tail and proportionately long legs. Serval are rather bigger than domestic cats but slimmer in build with a more upright posture. Body patterns vary, with streaking as well as spotting present. Black serval occur in some highland areas of the region.

Habits
Mainly nocturnal and solitary but occasionally active during the day. Serval hide up in the cover of tall grass, reeds or shrubs. Rats and mice form the bulk of their diet. They often hunt in wet or swampy areas avoided by other predators, where frogs may supplement the diet.

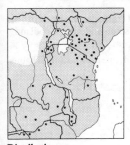

Habitat
Moist grasslands, reedbeds, riverine forest and well watered woodlands.

Where best seen
Apparently common in many wetland areas but not often seen on account of their nocturnal habits. More diurnal in Ngorongoro and common in the Aberdares where black forms seem to outnumber normal coloured serval.

Distribution

ORDER **Carnivores** Carnivora
FAMILY **Cats** Felidae

CARACAL *Felis caracal*
K: Simba mangu   F: Caracal   D: Wüstenluchs

Spoor 4 cm

Main colour	Shoulder height	Typical weight	Gestation period	Number of young
Russet	40 cm, 1'4"	15 kg, 33 lb	65 days	1–5

Description
A medium-sized cat, a little smaller in height than the serval but more solidly built. Coat colour is an even pinkish tan but this varies regionally. The underparts are paler. Caracal have short tails and prominently tufted ears which are characteristic. Similar in appearance to the European lynx but a different species.

Habits
Almost totally nocturnal and therefore very rarely seen. Caracal are solitary and secretive. They hunt small mammals and birds and in some areas will prey upon sheep and goats.

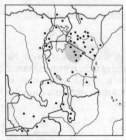

Habitat
Very widely spread through semi-desert, dry savanna, thornbush scrub and open woodland.

Where best seen
Not often encountered, due to its nocturnal habits.

Distribution

ORDER **Carnivores** Carnivora
FAMILY **Cats** Felidae

GOLDEN CAT *Felis aurata*
F: Chat doré   D: Goldkatze

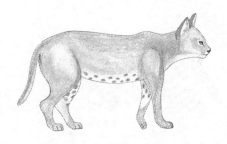

Main colour	Shoulder height	Number of
Fawn	40 cm, 1′4″	young 1

Description
Very similar in general appearance to the caracal but lacking the tufted ears. Golden cat are a little smaller than caracal. Coat colour varies from chestnut through golden to grey-brown. Characteristic is the spotted white belly.

Habits
Nocturnal, solitary and secretive.

Habitat
A forest species occurring in East Africa in highland forest and mountain moorland and in lowland forest in central and west Africa.

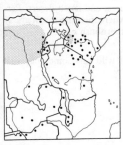

Where best seen
Rarely seen in the region but reputedly less uncommon in the Ruwenzoris.

Distribution

ORDER **Carnivores** Carnivora
FAMILY **Cats** Felidae

AFRICAN WILD CAT *Felis lybica*
K: Paka pori   F: Chat sauvage   D: Falbkatze

Spoor
3.5 cm

Main colour	Shoulder height	Typical weight	Gestation period	Number of
Grey brown	30 cm, 1'	5 kg, 11 lb	65 days	young 2–4

Description
The wild cat is very like a domestic cat in size and shape. It has a grey or sandy coat, striped to a greater or lesser extent on the sides and flanks. It has a ringed tail.

Habits
Generally nocturnal, though sometimes seen during the day. Secretive and solitary. Wild cats prey on rats, mice and birds.

Habitat
The wild cat occurs in a wide variety of habitats over much of Africa, excluding only true forest and harsh desert. Perhaps most often seen where there are rough grassy areas with plenty of thornbush cover.

Where best seen
Infrequently seen but wild cats sometimes visit camps after dark.

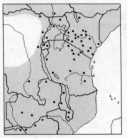
Distribution

ORDER **Carnivores** Carnivora
FAMILY **Cat-like mammals** Viverridae

AFRICAN CIVET *Civettictis civetta*
K: Fungo   F: Civette   D: Zibetkatze

Photo: page 50

Spoor
4.5 cm

Main colour	Shoulder height	Typical weight	Gestation period	Number of young
Grey	40 cm, 1'4"	13 kg, 28 lb	65 days	2–4

Description
Although often called a cat, the civet is in fact related to the mongooses. It does, nevertheless, have a cat-like appearance. It has black and white 'panda' markings around the eyes and a distinctively striped and spotted coat. Overall colour is grey. It is rather larger and bulkier than a domestic cat and much more heavily built than the genet.

Habits
Civets are largely nocturnal and terrestrial. They are almost invariably solitary. They move slowly and purposefully, feeding on a wide variety of items including insects, fruit, reptiles, birds and vegetable matter.

Habitat
Moist savanna and forest areas where water is available. Good cover along watercourses seems to be the preferred habitat.

Where best seen
Not often seen anywhere but civet are reasonably common in suitable locations throughout their range.

Distribution

ORDER **Carnivores** Carnivora
FAMILY **Cat-like mammals** Viverridae

TREE CIVET *Nandinia binotata*
F: Nandinie   D: Pardelroller

Spoor
3.5 cm

Main colour	Length	Typical weight	Gestation period	Number of
Fawn	90 cm, 3′	2 kg, 4.5 lb	65 days	young 2–3

Description
The tree, or palm, civet looks much like a genet but is a little larger, a more sandy colour, has much smaller ears and less well defined markings. The tail, which is not fully ringed, takes up half the creature's total length.

Habits
Solitary and nocturnal, spending most of its time high in forest trees. Diet consists of fruit, birds, rats and mice.

Habitat
Confined to true forests. Occurs in montane forests, lowland rain forests and drier savanna forest.

Where best seen
Rarely seen.

Distribution

ORDER **Carnivores** Carnivora
FAMILY **Cat-like mammals** Viverridae

LARGE SPOTTED GENET *Genetta tigrina*
SMALL SPOTTED GENET *Genetta genetta*
K: Kanu   F: Genette   D: Ginsterkatze

Photo: page 51

Large spotted

Small spotted

Spoor
2.5 cm

Main colour	Length	Typical weight	Gestation period	Number of young
Grey brown	1 m, 3'4"	2 kg, 4.5 lb	75 days	2–4

Description
Small, slender, cat-like creatures with spotted or blotched coats and long, ringed tails. The genets are in fact more closely related to mongooses than to cats. The large spotted genet has a black tip to its tail while the slightly smaller small spotted genet has a white tip. Coat markings and colouration are variable and some doubt exists about the exact relationship between the various genet species and races.

Habits
Nocturnal creatures active in the early hours of darkness as well as in the early morning. Genet prey on rodents, small birds and other small creatures. They may become very tame in well frequented areas, prowling between table legs at dinner in certain lodges and around fires in camp sites.

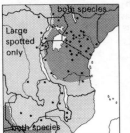

Habitat
Bushy and wooded areas, especially along watercourses. The large spotted genet tends to favour more forested areas while the small spotted is less tied to waterways and may be found in more arid places.

Where best seen
Often seen around lodges and camps after dark throughout its range.

Distribution

ORDER **Carnivores** Carnivora
FAMILY **Mongooses** Viverridae

WHITE TAILED MONGOOSE *Ichneumia albicauda*
K: Nguchiro   F: Mangouste à queue blanche   D: Weissschwanzichneumon

Spoor
4 cm

Main colour	Length	Typical weight	Number of
Grey	1.1 m, 3'6"	4.5 kg, 10 lb	young 1–3

Description
This is the largest of the mongooses though it is a little less heavily built than the large grey mongoose. Overall colouring is pale brown to grey and the bushy white tail is characteristic. Melanistic animals occur in some areas and these have a pure black tail.

Habits
The white tailed mongoose is nocturnal, solitary or in pairs. Diet consists of frogs, mice, birds, insects and vegetable matter.

Habitat
White tailed mongooses occur in a variety of grassy and wooded habitats with a preference for well watered areas.

Where best seen
At night, often scavenges around lodges and camps throughout its range.

Distribution

ORDER **Carnivores** Carnivora
FAMILY **Mongooses** Viverridae

LARGE GREY MONGOOSE *Herpestes ichneumon*
K: Nguchiro   F: Mangouste grise   D: Greiichneumon

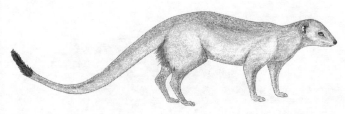

Spoor
4 cm

Main colour	Length	Typical weight	Number of young
Grey	1 m, 3'4"	3.5 kg, 8 lb	1–3

Description
Another large mongoose, more heavily built than the white tailed but generally shorter in overall length. Colouring is similar, brown or greyish, but the long slender tail is tipped with a black bristle.

Habits
The large grey mongoose is more of a diurnal species but otherwise has similar habits to the white tailed.

Habitat
Occurs most commonly in riverine and wetland fringes where reedbeds and rank herbage provide good cover.

Where best seen
Scattered in suitable locations throughout its range.

Distribution

ORDER **Carnivores** Carnivora
FAMILY **Mongooses** Viverridae

MARSH or WATER MONGOOSE *Atilax paludinosus*
K: Nguchiro: F: Mangouste des marais   D: Sumpfichneumon

Spoor
4 cm

Main colour	Length	Typical weight	Number of
Brown	80 cm, 2′8″	3 kg, 7 lb	young 1–2

Description
This is a largish mongoose with a furry brown coat. It may appear somewhat otter-like, especially when seen in water, but it has a more pointed nose than the otters.

Habits
The water mongoose is most active during early mornings and in the evening. It feeds mainly on frogs, toads, mice and crabs. Mainly solitary.

Habitat
Closely associated with rivers and wetland fringes where there is adjacent cover of reeds or rank herbage. Also found along seasonal streams.

Where best seen
Widely scattered in suitable locations throughout its range.

Distribution

ORDER **Carnivores** Carnivora
FAMILY **Mongooses** Viverridae

MELLER'S MONGOOSE *Rhynchogale melleri*
K: Nguchiro   F: Mangouste de Meller   D: Mellermaushund

Spoor
3 cm

Main colour	Length	Typical weight	Number of
Light brown	80 cm, 2'7"	2.5 kg, 5 lb 8 oz	young 1–3

Description
A largish mongoose coloured light brown. It has a characteristic furry tail which may be tipped black, brown or white. It is generally lighter in appearance than the white tailed mongoose.

Habits
Meller's mongoose is generally solitary and nocturnal. Its diet consists mainly of termites though other insects and fruit may be taken.

Habitat
This species is associated with open woodland or grassy savanna where there are suitable termite colonies to supply its food requirements.

Where best seen
An uncommon species whose distribution and status is imperfectly known. Confined to the southern parts of Zaïre, Zambia and Malaŵi.

Distribution

ORDER **Carnivores** Carnivora
FAMILY **Mongooses** Viverridae

SELOUS' MONGOOSE *Paracynictis selousi*
K: Nguchiro F: Mangouste de Selous D: Selousmaushund

Spoor
3 cm

Main colour	Length	Typical weight	Number of
Grey brown	75 cm, 2'6"	1.7 kg, 3lb 12 oz	young 1–4

Description
A medium-sized mongoose which is grey or grey brown in colour and has a white tipped tail.

Habits
Mainly solitary and nocturnal, lying up during the day in burrows excavated in sandy soils. They will dig for food if necessary and the diet consists mainly of insects, larvae, scorpions and small reptiles, mammals or birds.

Habitat
Open scrub and woodland savanna where there is sandy soil.

Where best seen
Confined within the region to Zambia and Malawi. This species is not common.

Distribution

ORDER **Carnivores** Carnivora
FAMILY **Mongooses** Viverridae

BUSHY TAILED MONGOOSE *Bdeogale crassicauda*
K: Nguchiro   F: Mangouste à queue touffue   D: Buschschwanzichneumon

Main colour	Length	Typical weight
Grey brown	70 cm, 2'3"	1.6 kg, 3 lb 8 oz

Description
This is a largish mongoose coloured sandy grey to grey brown. It has a characteristic drooping bushy tail. This is a very rare species in this region.

Habits
Solitary and nocturnal and known only from a handful of specimens.

Habitat
Woodland, grassy savanna and rocky outcrops.

Where best seen
Very rare in the region and unlikely to be encountered.

Distribution

ORDER **Carnivores** Carnivora
FAMILY **Mongooses** Viverridae

SLENDER MONGOOSE *Galerella sanguinea*
K: Nguchiro   F: Mangouste rouge   D: Rotichneumon

 Spoor
3 cm

Main colour	Length	Typical weight	Gestation period	Number of young
Fawn	60 cm, 2'	600 g, 20 oz	45 days	2

Description
The slender mongoose has a lithe, slim appearance and the tail has a distinctive black tip. Overall colour is a plain golden tan to greyish brown. Sometimes called the black tipped mongoose.

Habits
This species is diurnal. The slender mongoose tends to be solitary and is often seen scampering across the road. It feeds on mice and lizards, supplemented with beetles and grubs.

Habitat
The slender mongoose occurs in a very wide range of habitats except desert.

Where best seen
Reasonably common throughout the region.

Distribution

ORDER **Carnivores** Carnivora
FAMILY **Mongooses** Viverridae

BANDED MONGOOSE *Mungos mungo*
K: Nguchiro F: Mangouste rayée D: Zebra manguste

Spoor 3 cm

Main colour	Length	Typical weight	Gestation period	Number of
Grey	60 m, 2′	1.5 kg, 3 lb 6 oz	60 days	young 2–6

Description
A short, chubby mongoose, grey in colour with a series of black bands across the back and partly around the body. It has a hunched-back appearance and a scampering gait.

Habits
Another diurnal mongoose. The banded mongoose lives in colonies of up to 30 individuals and they forage together amongst dead vegetation and fallen branches, feeding on beetles, grubs and other insects.

Habitat
The banded mongoose prefers areas of substantial undergrowth in dry wooded savanna regions.

Where best seen
Suitable habitat throughout the range.

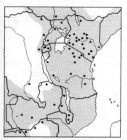
Distribution

ORDER **Carnivores** Carnivora
FAMILY **Mongooses** Viverridae

DWARF MONGOOSE *Helogale parvula*
K: Kitafe   F: Mangouste nain   D: Zwergichneumon

Spoor
2 cm

Main colour	Length	Typical weight	Gestation period	Number of
Fawn	40 cm, 1'4"	270 g, 10 oz	45 days	young 2–6

Description
The dwarf mongoose is the smallest of all the mongooses. It is brown to yellowish-grey with a bare, pinkish nose that is visible at close quarters. An uncommon but closely related species *H. hirtula* occurs in northern Kenya.

Habits
Dwarf mongooses live in colonies in holes excavated into termite mounds. They are often seen sunning themselves on these mounds or peeking from their holes. Diet consists of termites, beetles and grubs.

Habitat
Dry savanna where suitable termite mounds exist.

Where best seen
Common in suitable terrain throughout their range.

Distribution

ORDER **Carnivores** Carnivora
FAMILY **Mustelidae**

CLAWLESS OTTER *Aonyx capensis*
SPOTTED NECKED OTTER *Lutra maculicollis*

K: Fisi maji F: Loutre à joues blanches, Loutre à cou tacheté
D: Fingerotter, Fleckenhalsotter

Clawless otter   Spotted necked otter

Spoor 4 cm

Main colour	Length	Typical weight	Gestation period	Number of
Brown	Clawless: 1.3 m, 4'3"	Clawless: 14 kg, 30 lb	60 days	young 2–3
	Spotted necked: 1 m, 3'4"	Spotted necked: 5 kg, 11 lb		

Description
Long, sleek, sinuous animals that are most often seen in or near water. The clawless otter is the larger of the two and is variously coloured fawn to dark brown with pale underparts. The pale throat distinguishes it from the rather smaller spotted necked otter which is heavily spotted on the throat. The colour of this species is generally darker and it is slighter in build. Otters differ from mongooses in the rounded appearance of their faces and noses and in having webbed feet.

Habits
The clawless otter is active mornings and evenings, spending most of its time in water, although it may wander some distance away. The spotted necked otter is more closely tied to waterways. It is mainly solitary but sometimes found in small groups. Both species eat frogs, fish and crabs.

Distribution

Habitat
Permanent bodies of water. The clawless otter is also found in the sea in some areas, though it does require access to fresh water. It is less confined to water than the spotted necked otter and finds its way along small streams and even dry watercourses. The spotted necked otter is associated with large lakes in this region.

Where best seen
Not often seen as otters are generally shy creatures. The clawless otter occurs on many waterways, especially in Kenya and Tanzania, and the spotted necked otter occurs in Lake Victoria.

ORDER **Carnivores** Carnivora
FAMILY **Mustelidae**

HONEY BADGER or RATEL *Mellivora capensis*
K: Nyegere   F: Ratel   D: Hönigdachs

Spoor
10 cm

Main colour	Shoulder height	Typical weight	Gestation period	Number of young
Black and white	26 m, 10"	12 kg, 26 lb	180 days	2

Description
A low, flat-backed animal characteristically marked with a pinkish to pale grey back and crown contrasting with a black face and underparts. The feet are equipped with long tough claws. Honey badgers look rather sleek but in fact possess a thick, loosely hanging skin which renders them almost immune to attack.

Habits
Mainly nocturnal but sometimes seen during the day. Usually solitary and shy but can be quite aggressive. Reported to be able to hold their own against much larger animals. Diet includes scorpions, mice, insects, birds and snakes with honey forming only a small part of their diet.

Habitat
Found in almost every habitat throughout Africa.

Where best seen
Open plains such as the short grass areas of the Serengeti.

Distribution

ORDER **Carnivores** Carnivora
FAMILY **Mustelidae**

STRIPED POLECAT or ZORILLA *Ictonyx striatus*
STRIPED WEASEL *Poecilogale albinucha*

K: Kicheche F: Zorille, Belette D: Zorilla, Mauswiesel

Zorilla   Striped weasel

Spoor
2 cm

Main colour	Length	Typical weight	Gestation period	Number of
Black and white	Polecat: 60 cm, 2'	Polecat: 850 g, 1 lb 4 oz	40 days	young 1–3
	Weasel: 45 cm, 1'6"	Weasel: 250 g, 9 oz		

Description
These two species have very similar and easily recognisable colouring. The striped polecat, or zorilla, is the larger of the two and is more robustly built. It has a furrier appearance. The striped weasel is small and sinuous. Both have black faces and undersides with a vividly streaked black and white back and tail. The crown of the weasel is whiter than that of the polecat.

Habits
Both species are rather uncommon, nocturnal and solitary. Very little is known about the striped weasel. The striped polecat is occasionally encountered. It lives in burrows and feeds on insects and mice.

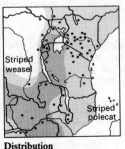

Habitat
The striped polecat lives in almost any habitat from desert to forest while the striped weasel inhabits mainly grassland savanna.

Where best seen
Neither species is seen very often.

Distribution

ORDER **Primates**
FAMILY **Apes** Pongidae

MOUNTAIN GORILLA *Gorilla gorilla*
K: Makaku   F: Gorille   D: Gorilla

Photo: pages 41, 51

Main colour	Overall height	Typical weight	Gestation period	Number of young
Black	1.5 m, 5'	135 kg, 300 lb	250 days	1

Description
An unmistakable, huge, black, furry creature growing up to 1.5m or 5' in height. Enormous girth, especially in older males, which also develop prominent brow ridges and extended craniums. 'Silverback' males possess a mantle of silver or grey hair on the upper part of the back. The face, palms and soles are leathery but the whole of the rest of the body is covered in thick fur. The arms are rather longer than the legs. Females tend to be smaller than males. The mountain gorilla is rather larger and has thicker fur than the more abundant lowland gorilla which occurs in central and west Africa. It is an endangered species.

Habits
Gorillas are diurnal and follow a daily routine. They browse for much of the day on leaves, shoots and vegetable matter, lying up during the midday hours. At dusk, they make 'nests' of broken saplings or bamboo in which they spend the night. Gorillas stay together in family units of 6 – 12 animals although there is a certain interchange of members between groups. They are strongly territorial and unless 'habituated' to humans, will act aggressively to an intruder.

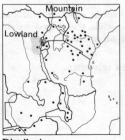
Distribution

Habitat
Mountain forest, especially bamboo, around 8000' on certain ranges in east central Africa. Habitat destruction has added to poaching to cause a serious decline in numbers.

Where best seen
Mountain gorillas have been habituated to visitors in Volcanoes and still occur in small numbers in the far south west of Uganda. Eastern lowland gorillas may be seen in Kahuzi-Biega.

ORDER **Primates**
FAMILY **Apes** Pongidae

CHIMPANZEE *Pan troglodytes*
K: Soko   F: Chimpanzé   D: Grosschimpanse

Main colour	Overall height	Typical weight	Gestation period	Number of young
Black	1.3 m, 4'3"	45 kg, 100 lb	230 days	1

Description
Rather smaller than the gorilla but nevertheless a large ape. Black in colour and covered all over in thick fur except for the face, palms and soles which are bare. The head is rounder than that of the gorilla with more prominent ears. Arms are rather longer than the legs. There is no tail. The smaller but otherwise similar pigmy chimpanzee occurs south and west of the Zaïre River.

Habits
Chimpanzees occur in family groups and are diurnal. Unlike the gorilla, they spend much of their time clambering about in the branches of trees although they do forage on the ground as well. They feed on a variety of leaves and vegetable matter. Chimps are able to walk upright but often move on all fours.

Distribution

Habitat
A variety of forests, especially at lower altitude, throughout much of central and western Africa.

Where best seen
Probably the best chance is at Gombe Stream, where they are accustomed to visitors but chimpanzees are not uncommon in western Uganda, western Tanzania and throughout much of Zaïre.

ORDER **Primates**
FAMILY **Monkeys** Cercopithecidae

OLIVE BABOON *Papio anubis*
YELLOW BABOON *Papio cynocephalus*
CHACMA BABOON *Papio ursinus*

K: Nyani F: Babouin D: Pavian

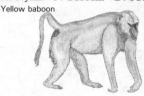
Yellow baboon

Olive baboon

Spoor
15 cm

Main colour	Length	Typical weight	Gestation period	Number of young
Grey brown	1.3 m, 4'2"	Male: 30 kg, 65 lb Female: 18 kg, 40 lb	185 days	1

Description
Heavily built monkeys with elongated dog-like muzzles and long drooping tails. The olive baboon is the largest and develops a full mane of fur around the upper part of the body. This is especially noticeable in older males. The yellow baboon has a much sparser growth of fur and is a little lighter in build. Colouring is fairly well indicated by the names, the olive baboon being a distinctly greenish shade of brown-grey while the yellow is a yellowish brown. Colouring does vary with age, however. The more slimly built chacma baboon occurs in the southern part of the region. There seem to be areas of overlap between the species and some hybridisation takes place.

Habits
Baboons are gregarious animals, occurring in troops of 30 – 100 individuals. They emerge at dawn to forage and are active throughout the day, though less so at noon. Their daily routine usually includes a visit to water. They roost at night in trees or on high rocky ledges. Diet includes fruit, grass, roots, insects and small mammals such as young antelope. Baboons often mix with grazing antelope. They post a sentry at the top of a nearby tree, who will give a characteristic gruff double bark as a warning. Predators such as leopard will cause a frenzy of blood curdling screaming.

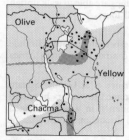
Distribution

Habitat
A wide variety of savanna woodlands and hillsides where there is access to water.

Where best seen
Difficult to avoid on safari as they become quickly accustomed to camps and lodges and will boldly raid rubbish bins, dinner tables, tents and vehicles. The yellow baboon occurs generally east of the Great Rift Valley and the chacma in the south.

ORDER **Primates**
FAMILY **Monkeys** Cercopithecidae

SYKES', BLUE and GOLDEN MONKEYS
Cercopithecus mitis
L'HOEST'S MONKEY *Cercopithecus l'hoesti*

K: Kima F: Cercopithècus à diadème D: Diademmeerkatze

Syke's monkey   Blue monkey

Spoor

Main colour	Length	Typical weight	Gestation period	Number of young
Grey brown	1.3 m, 4'3"	Male: 9 kg, 20 lb Female: 5 kg, 11 lb	125 days	1

Description
Medium-sized, well-proportioned monkeys that occur in a wide range of colour forms throughout much of eastern and southern Africa. Generally they have tufted eyebrows and cheeks, often white, giving an 'old man' appearance. Blue monkeys are a grey-blue to black in colour. They are called samango monkeys in the south of the region although some authorities classify these as a separate species *C. albogularis*.

Sykes' monkeys are a speckled golden colour on the back and head with the limbs and face bluish and a prominent white ring around the throat and on the chest. A further variety of this form is called the golden monkey. This is a brighter, almost orange colour with black limbs.

The related L'Hoest's monkey is larger, an even dark brown to black with white patches on its face and throat.

Habits
These monkeys are diurnal and live in groups. They spend much of their time in trees but also forage on the ground. They have a rather bird-like hooting call. Diet consists of leaves, flowers, roots and berries and a variety of fruits.

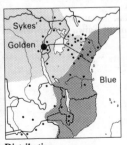

Distribution

Habitat
A variety of forested areas from sea level to 7000' in altitude.

Where best seen
Widely distributed in suitable forest areas, some close to urban areas. Blue monkeys occur generally in the east of the region and in coastal areas. Sykes' monkeys are found in the western parts of the region. The golden monkey is restricted to highland forest on the Uganda-Zäire border area. L'Hoest's monkey occurs in the forested zone as far east as Rwanda and southern Uganda.

ORDER **Primates**
FAMILY **Monkeys** Cercopithecidae

DE BRAZZA'S MONKEY *Cercopithecus neglectus*
F: Cercopithèque de Brazza   D: Brazza meerkatze

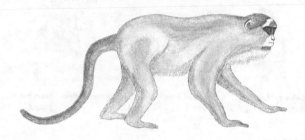

Main colour	Length	Typical weight	Gestation period	Number of
Grey	1.2 m, 4′	Male: 7 kg, 15 lb Female: 4 kg, 9 lb	180 days	young 1

Description
This is a relatively heavily built monkey. Coat colour is blue grey with a white rump. The main characteristic features, however, are a bright orange forehead and a pure white beard which render the species unmistakable.

Habits
An extremely shy creature which is, therefore, rarely seen. De Brazza's monkeys live in trees in small bands. Unlike other species, if alarmed they do not call or flee but remain quietly stationary.

Habitat
This species inhabits the dense canopy of forest trees.

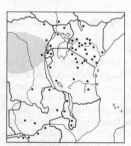

Distribution

Where best seen
Generally uncommon, occurring sparsely in western Kenya, including Saiwa Swamp, and in Uganda and Zaïre.

ORDER **Primates**
FAMILY **Monkeys** Cercopithecidae

WHITE NOSED MONKEY *Cercopithecus nictitans*
F: Hocheur D: Weissnase

Main colour	Length	Typical weight	Number of young
Grey brown	1.3 m, 4′2″	6 kg, 13 lb	1

Description
Also called the copper or red tailed monkey, this species is very like a small Sykes' monkey in general appearance. It is dark yellowish-brown above, pale underneath, with white cheeks. The most noticeable feature is, however, a clown-like white blob on the nose. The skin around the eyes is blue and the latter half of the tail is bright chestnut.

Habits
This is a species that spends most of its time in trees and lives in groups.

Habitat
A forest species.

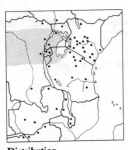

Where best seen
Not uncommon in forests of western Kenya, north western Tanzania, Uganda and Zaïre.

Distribution

169

ORDER **Primates**
FAMILY **Monkeys** Cercopithecidae

VERVET MONKEY *Cercopithecus aethiops*
K: Tumbili   F: Grivet   D: Grünmeerkatze

Spoor
5 cm

Main colour	Length	Typical weight	Gestation period	Number of young
Yellowish grey	1.1 m, 3'6"	5 kg, 11 lb	180 days	1

Description
A lightly built monkey with a yellowish brown colouring, sometimes tending to olive. The underparts are white and the face is black, characteristically edged with white. The long tail is tipped black. The scrotum of older males is rather startlingly coloured turquoise.

Habits
These monkeys live in troops of up to 30 animals and spend their days foraging both in trees and on the ground. Diet is a wide variety of leaves, flowers and fruits. Like baboons, they quickly become accustomed to humans and can become quite aggressive, snatching anything edible from people's hands.

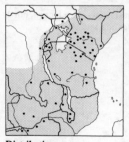

Habitat
A variety of well watered savanna woodlands, especially close to rivers.

Where best seen
Common in many areas of the region.

Distribution

ORDER **Primates**
FAMILY **Monkeys** Cercopithecidae

PATAS MONKEY *Erythrocebus patas*
F: Singe rouge D: Husarenaffe

Main colour	Length	Typical weight	Gestation period	Number of young
Sandy	1.8 m, 5'10"	10 kg, 22 lb	170 days	1

Description
A slimly built, almost spindly-looking monkey. Main colour is an ochreous yellow-orange with the undersides rather paler. The face is characteristically fringed with fur, giving a round appearance.

Habits
A monkey which may be solitary or found in small groups of up to 4 or 6 individuals. This species is quite shy and is easily overlooked. It is a terrestrial species and its colouring helps to conceal it. Patas monkeys often use termite hills as lookout points.

Habitat
Associated with drier thornbush and woodland savanna.

Where best seen
Widespread but very local and not often seen. Occurs in the dry regions of north western Kenya and north eastern Uganda. Reported to be not uncommon on ranchland in the Laikipia district of Kenya.

Distribution

ORDER **Primates**
FAMILY **Monkeys** Cercopithecidae

BLACK AND WHITE COLOBUS *Colobus polykomos, Colobus abyssinicus*

K: Mbega F: Colobe blanc et noir D: Weissbartstummelaffe **Photo:** page 41

Main colour	Length	Typical weight	Gestation period	Number of
Black and white	1.8 m, 5'10"	12 kg, 26 lb	150 days	young 1

Description
An attractive monkey, basically black but with a fringed mantle of long white fur. There is a more or less pronounced fringe of white around the face and the tail has a bushy white tip. Colobus do not possess thumbs on their hands. The various species of black and white colobus differ in the amount of white hair, especially around the face. There is some disagreement amongst authorities on the names of these species with *C. guereza* and *C. angolensis* sometimes used instead of the Latin names shown above.

Habits
The black and white colobus occurs in bands which in some areas may number up to 100 individuals. They spend most of their time high in forest trees although they do come to the ground at times, for example to visit waterholes. They are remarkably agile, almost flying from tree to tree, when their long white hair streams magnificently behind them. Diet consists of leaves. Colobus emit a loud croaking call, especially at dawn, which reverberates for great distances.

Distribution

Habitat
A variety of forests from sea level to 10 000'. There seems to be a preference for forest edges and areas where there are grassy clearings. Destruction of forests threatens the colobus in some areas.

Where best seen
Colobus polykomos occurs in western Uganda, parts of Tanzania and on the East African coast. *C. abyssinicus* can be seen in many highland forests of Kenya. They are common and easily seen in the Aberdares salient.

ORDER **Primates**
FAMILY **Monkeys** Cercopithecidae

RED COLOBUS *Colobus badius*
F: Colobe bai   D: Roter stummelaffe

Main colour	Length	Typical weight	Gestation period	Number of young
Russet	1.3 m, 4'2"	10 kg, 22 lb	160 days	1

Description
General colouring is reddish brown with a brighter, almost orange crown. Underparts are paler and the tail is nearly black. There are many variations and sub-species of red colobus and colouring varies significantly from area to area.

Habits
As the appearance of different forms of red colobus vary, so do their habits. Some are highly gregarious such as those from parts of Tanzania and Uganda which live in groups of up to 50 individuals. In Kenya, the rather different Tana River red colobus lives in much smaller groups. They are generally an arboreal species.

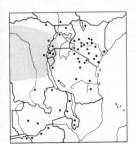

Habitat
Coastal, riverine and mountain rain forests.

Where best seen
An uncommon species, much rarer, for example, than the black and white colobus. It is patchily distributed across the region with races and sub-species quite isolated from each other.

Distribution

ORDER **Primates**
FAMILY **Monkeys** Cercopithecidae

BLACK MANGABEY *Cercocebus albigena, cercocebus galeritus*
F: Mangabé noir   D: Schopfemangabe

Main colour	Length	Typical weight	Number of young
Black	1.3 m, 4'2"	10 kg, 22 lb	1

Description
A dark brown to black monkey with tufty eyebrows and a characteristic crest on the crown. The tail is rather scruffy looking and this is another distinguishing feature. The related Tana River mangabey is greyer in colour and slightly smaller. Another mangabey, the grey cheeked, occurs in Rwanda and Zaïre.

Habits
Mangabeys live in groups and are generally arboreal.

Habitat
A forest species. The Tana River mangabey is confined to the Tana River Primate Reserve in eastern Kenya where it lives in the riverine forest.

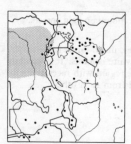

Distribution

Where best seen
Locally distributed in suitable forests in Uganda, western Tanzania, Rwanda and Zaïre.

ORDER **Primates**
FAMILY **Bushbabies** Lorisidae

POTTO *Perodicticus potto*
K: Potto   F: Potto   D: Potto

Main colour	Length	Typical weight
Grey brown	45 cm, 1'6"	1 kg, 2 lb 3 oz

Description
The potto is a chubby little creature, very like a bushbaby but with a much shorter tail. It is covered with dense fur and coloured grey to sandy brown. All members of this family possess large eyes which are designed for nocturnal use and are highly reflective.

Habits
A slow, ponderous creature. Nocturnal and confined to trees. Pottos are usually solitary.

Habitat
Confined to rain forest areas.

Where best seen
Occurs in western Kenya and Uganda where it may be located after dark by torchlight which reflects strongly in its eyes.

Distribution

ORDER **Primates**
FAMILY **Bushbabies** Lorisidae

THICK TAILED BUSHBABY *Galago crassicaudatus*
F: Galago à queue épaisse   D: Riesengalago

Main colour	Length	Typical weight	Gestation period	Number of
Grey	73 cm, 2'5"	1.2 kg, 2 lb 10 oz	135 days	young 2

Description
This species of bushbaby has a long bushy tail. It is also called the greater galago and sometimes referred to simply as bushbaby. It is pale grey in colour. Ears are prominent, but less so than on the lesser bushbaby. The thick tailed bushbaby has large eyes.

Habits
Totally nocturnal and often solitary, though sometimes found in small groups of 3 – 4 animals. They normally remain high in trees. Diet consists of fruit, gum and insects. These bushbabies call at night with a noisy, baby-like squeal.

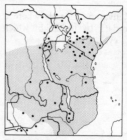

Habitat
Generally in areas of rain forest, from the coast to 7000'.

Where best seen
Locally common and may be seen by torchlight at night. Not infrequently seen along the East African coast where it may feed on the flowers of baobab trees.

Distribution

ORDER **Primates**
FAMILY **Bushbabies** Lorisidae

LESSER BUSHBABY *Galago senegalensis*
K: Komba   F: Galago de Senegal   D: Steppengalago

Main colour	Length	Typical weight	Gestation period	Number of young
Grey	37 cm, 1'3"	150 g, 5 oz	125 days	2

Description
An attractive little creature, much smaller and more slimly built than the thick tailed bushbaby but with more prominent ears. The tail is thin. Colouring is grey brown. Similarly large eyes. The still smaller Demidoff's bushbaby is found in western Uganda and Zaïre.

Habits
Very much like its larger relative, the lesser bushbaby is strictly nocturnal and spends its life in trees. Diet consists of gum and insects associated with the acacia trees where this species is often found. The lesser bushbaby is renowned for its leaping ability and will jump away from light if caught in a beam.

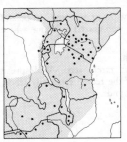

Habitat
The lesser bushbaby occurs in a variety of savanna woodlands, often being associated with particular types of trees such as acacia.

Where best seen
May be spotted after dark in many parts of the region.

Distribution

ORDER **Tubulidentata**
FAMILY **Orycteropodidae**

AARDVARK *Orycteropus afer*
K: Muhanga   F: Fourmillier   D: Erdferkel

Spoor
9 cm

Main colour	Length	Typical weight	Gestation period	Number of young
Grey brown	1.6 m, 5'3"	52 kg, 115 lb	210 days	1

Description
The aardvark, or antbear, is a hump-backed animal with an elongated pig-like snout, huge rabbit-like ears and a long tapering tail. It is a pale yellowish brown colour. The feet are equipped with long digging claws.

Habits
This is a solitary species and predominantly nocturnal. Diet consists of termites and ants which are licked up with the creature's long sticky tongue. The aardvark is a powerful and rapid digger and lives underground in extensive burrows.

Habitat
Mainly associated with grassy and woodland savanna, especially well-grazed savanna where termites also occur.

Where best seen
Not uncommon but rarely seen. Widespread throughout much of the region especially where there are termite mounds.

Distribution

ORDER **Pholidota**
FAMILY **Manidae**

PANGOLIN *Manis temminckii, Manis gigantea*
K: Kakukuona F: Pangolin D: Schuppentier

Spoor
5 cm

Main colour	Length	Typical weight	Gestation period	Number of young
Brown	80 cm, 2'8"	7 kg, 15 lb	150 days	1

Description
A hump-backed, long-tailed creature with a reptilian appearance. It is covered with thick overlapping scales. The head is pointed, giving an almost symmetrical silhouette. Claws are long and curved. The giant pangolin is very similar in appearance but is rather larger. It occurs in the western parts of the region.

Habits
The pangolin is another solitary and nocturnal species. Its powerful claws may be used to dig for termites and ants which form its diet. Pangolin do not dig deep burrows like the aardvark but hide during the day among debris, thick bushes and fallen branches. They walk on their hind feet, are slow moving and will roll into balls when disturbed. Pangolin, especially the giant species, climb trees using their claws to grip on to the bark.

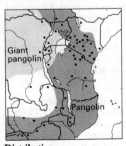

Habitat
The pangolin is mainly associated with grassy and woodland savanna as well as floodplains. The giant pangolin is much more strongly associated with true forest.

Where best seen
Very rarely encountered except by chance. Although widespread throughout the region, pangolin of both species are quite uncommon.

Distribution

ORDER **Rodentia**
FAMILY **Porcupines** Hystricidae

PORCUPINE *Hystrix africae-australis, Hystrix cristata*
K: Nungu   F: Porc-épique   D: Stachelschwein

Spoor 9 cm

Main colour	Length	Typical weight	Gestation period	Number of
Grey	85 cm, 2'7"	18 kg, 40 lb	55 days	young 1–4

Description
Porcupines are large rodents with unmistakable black and white spines covering the back and tail. The tail is tipped with a 'rattle' of hollow spines. The face, legs and lower body are covered in hair and are black in colour. The head and nape of the neck has a crest of long black hairs. The difference between the two species is not obvious to the casual observer. In *Hystrix cristata* the rattle quills are shorter and the rump is blackish. *Hystrix africae-australis* has a white centre to the rump.

Habits
Porcupines are mainly solitary and nocturnal. They forage at night with a lumbering gait, the quills and rattles scraping as they move. The spines and the hairs on the crest are normally carried unerected but can be raised at will and rattled aggressively. This appears to double the size of the animal. Rather than flee, porcupines will try to reverse towards a predator and lion have been seen with quills stuck into their faces. Generally, however, porcupines will freeze or run off at surprising speed if disturbed. Diet consists of roots, tubers and fruits.

Distribution

Habitat
Most habitats except dense forest and wetlands. Porcupines require cover in the form of rocks, crevices or holes in which to spend the day.

Where best seen
Common throughout East Africa but not often seen because of their nocturnal habits. *H. cristata* occurs in Kenya and Uganda as well as in northern Tanzania where it overlaps with *H. africae-australis* which replaces it to the south.

ORDER **Rodentia**
FAMILY **Canerats** Thryonomyidae

GREATER CANERAT *Thryonomys swinderianus*
LESSER CANERAT *Thryonomys gregorianus*
K: Ndezi F: Avlacode D: Rohrratte

Main colour	Length	Typical weight	Gestation period	Number of
Brown	Greater: 70 cm, 2'4" Lesser: 50 cm, 1'8"	Greater: 4 kg, 9 lb Lesser: 1.8 kg, 4 lb	150 days	young 2–6

Description
Large, rat-like creatures with a compact appearance and long slender tails. Colouring is an even mid-brown. The two species are very similar in appearance, differing primarily in size.

Habits
Canerats are mainly nocturnal, inhabiting reedbeds along watercourses. They feed on grasses and reeds. In many parts of Africa, canerats are hunted and form an important part of people's diets.

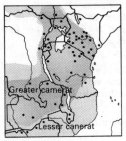

Distribution

Habitat
Reedbeds and dense grass alongside rivers, lakes and swamps. The greater canerat is never found far from water but the lesser canerat occurs also in drier areas. Canerats may also be found in cultivated areas such as sugar-cane plantations.

Where best seen
May be flushed from reedbeds. They are quite common around Lake Victoria. Both species occur throughout much of the region excepting the more arid zone of northern Kenya.

ORDER **Rodentia**
FAMILY **Squirrels** Sciuridae

GROUND SQUIRREL *Xerus erythropus, Xerus rutilus*
K: Kindi, kindiri F: Ecureuil foisseur D: Erdhörnchen **Photo:** page 52

Main colour	Length	Typical weight	Gestation period	Number of young
Grey	Striped: 50 cm, 1'8" Unstriped: 40 cm, 1'4"	650 g, 1 lb 6 oz	45 days	2–6

Description
These are the two commonly seen squirrels of the region. They are greyish in colour with bushy tails. The hind feet are slightly elongated compared with the forefeet. The difference between the species is that *Xerus erythropus* is a little larger and has a white stripe along the sides of the body. *Xerus rutilis* is plain grey.

Habits
Ground squirrels are confined to a terrestrial habitat, unlike the closely related tree squirrels. They live in loose colonies in a system of burrows. They are active by day and in hot areas will use their tails to shade themselves from the sun. They often sit upright and appear alert at all times. They feed on grass, seeds, leaves and insects.

Habitat
Both species are associated with dry sandy savanna areas. *Xerus rutilis* occurs in more arid locations and is common in northern Kenya.

Where best seen
Widespread and common in suitable areas throughout much of the region.

Distribution

182

ORDER **Rodentia**
FAMILY **Springhare** Pedetidae

SPRINGHARE *Pedetes capensis*
K: Kamendegere   F: Lièvre sauteur   D: Springhase

 Spoor
3 m

Main colour	Length	Typical weight	Gestation period	Number of
Fawn	80 cm, 2'8"	3 kg, 7 lb	80 days	young 1–2

Description
A large rodent which distinctly resembles a small kangaroo. It has elongated feet that are used for jumping. The face and ears are rather rabbit-like, hence the common name although springhares are not related to hares. The tail is longish, bushy and black tipped. Colouring is sandy. The short forelegs have claws adapted for digging.

Habits
Springhares are nocturnal. They live in colonies which inhabit extensive burrow systems dug into compacted sandy soils. They proceed by jumping and can be seen at night in the beam of a light when the reflection of the eyes seems to hop across the bush. They feed on grass.

Habitat
Short grass savanna with a sandy substrate. Absent from areas where the ground is too hard to burrow into.

Where best seen
Widespread throughout much of Kenya and Tanzania, as well as western Zambia, but local, occurring only in suitable areas.

Distribution

ORDER **Hares and rabbits** Lagomorpha
FAMILY **Leporidae**

AFRICAN HARE *Lepus capensis*
SCRUB HARE *Lepus saxatilis*
K: Sungura F: Lièvre D: Hase

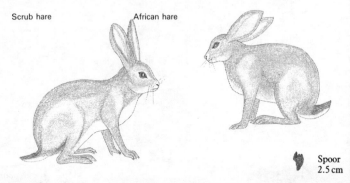

Scrub hare   African hare

Spoor 2.5 cm

Main colour	Length	Typical weight	Gestation period	Number of
Grey brown	55 cm, 1'10"	2 kg, 4 lb 8 oz	40 days	young 1–4

Description
These two species are very similar. They have the typical elongated ears and hind feet. General colouring is grey-brown with the belly white. The top of the tail is dark brown or black with the sides pale. The scrub hare is the larger of the two and has underparts which are purer white. The African hare may have buffy underparts.

Habits
Hares are grazers and generally active at night. They are largely solitary or occurring in pairs. Hares do not burrow like rabbits but lie up in grassy or scrub cover.

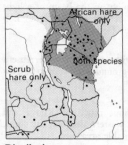

Habitat
The African hare inhabits short grass savanna and is associated with open areas. The scrub hare prefers woodland and thornbush scrub.

Where best seen
Widely spread in suitable localities throughout much of the region. The African hare does not occur in the south of the region while the scrub hare is absent only from the far north east of Kenya. Scrub hares may be flushed from the cover of their bushy habitat during the day.

Distribution

ORDER **Hares and rabbits** Lagomorpha
FAMILY **Leporidae**

BUNYORO RABBIT *Pronolagus marjorita*
RED ROCK RABBIT *Pronolagus rupestris*
F: Lapin sauvage D: Gras-hase

Main colour	Length	Typical weight	Gestation period	Number of
Grey brown	50 cm, 1'8"	1.7 kg, 3 lb 12 oz	35 days	young 1−2

Description
The main difference between rabbits and hares is that hares have hindlegs which are longer in relation to the forelegs than in rabbits. These species are smaller than the hares and have shorter ears. General colouring is yellowish-brown, paler underneath. The red rock rabbit has rufous feet and tail.

Habits
Nocturnal grazers, much like hares, except that rabbits dig burrows in which they spend the day.

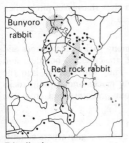

Distribution

Habitat
The Bunyoro rabbit occurs in open grasslands in western Uganda. The red rock rabbit inhabits areas of rocky hillside and koppies where there is a certain amount of vegetation.

Where best seen
The Bunyoro rabbit is locally common within its limited range in western Uganda. The red rock rabbit occurs in suitable parts of central Tanzania and western Kenya but is not often seen.

ORDER **Hyracoidea**
FAMILY **Hyraxes** Procavidae

ROCK HYRAX *Heterohyrax brucei, Procavia johnstoni* and *habessinica*
K: Pimbi   F: Daman de rocher   D: Klipschliefer   **Photo:** page 52

Spoor
3.5 cm

Main colour	Length	Typical weight	Gestation period	Number of
Grey brown	50 cm, 1'8"	3 kg, 7 lb	230 days	young 1–4

Description
Hyraxes are small rounded furry creatures with tiny bare ears and perky faces. General colouring is brown or grey with paler undersides. They possess a patch of contrasting hair in a short ridge along the mid-part of the spine. This is generally cream or yellowish. The various rock hyrax species may occur together and differ little in general appearance. The *Procavia* species tend to be a little larger and may have a black spot behind the ear. *Heterohyrax* is smaller and paler with a white spot over the eye. Although rodent-like in appearance, hyrax have the unlikely distinction of being more closely related to dugongs and elephant. Hyraxes are also called dassies in the southern part of the region.

Habits
Rock hyraxes are gregarious and are active by day. They may be seen sunning themselves in groups on rocky ledges and koppies. They eat a variety of leaves, grasses and fruits but appear to spend remarkably little time feeding. Rock hyraxes are preyed upon by leopards and by Verreaux' eagles whose distribution is closely tied to that of the hyrax. They make a restrained squeaking call which rises sharply in pitch when an eagle flies overhead.

Distribution

Habitat
Rock hyraxes live among rocky hills, gorges and koppies where there are crevices, boulders and suitable vegetation. They can squeeze into the most unlikely looking cracks and gaps in rocks where they hide from predators and from the heat of the sun.

Where best seen
Widespread throughout the region where suitable rocky outcrops occur.

ORDER **Hyracoidea**
FAMILY **Hyraxes** Procavidae

TREE HYRAX *Dendrohyrax arboreus, dorsalis and validus*
K: Pembere F: Daman d'arbre D: Baumschliefer

Main colour	Length	Typical weight	Gestation period	Number of young
Brown	50 cm, 1'8"	3 kg, 7 lb	210 days	1–3

Description
The tree hyraxes are similar in size, shape and general appearance to the rock hyraxes but have rather thicker and browner fur. The dorsal patch tends to be whiter in colour. *D. arboreus* is the typical East African form, with *D. dorsalis* replacing it to the west. *D. validus* occurs in the coastal regions.

Habits
Tree hyraxes, as their name implies, live mainly in trees. They are generally solitary and strictly nocturnal. Their most noticeable characteristic is their ear-shattering call which sounds like a comb being scraped over a microphone connected to a hundred watt amplifier. This call may be repeated at regular intervals through the night and allows widely separated individuals to maintain contact. Tree hyraxes may come to the ground and spend the day hidden in clumps of grass and dead branches.

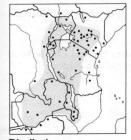

Habitat
Tree hyraxes are found in a wide range of moist forest and woodland areas including coastal, riverine and mountain forests.

Where best seen
Common in suitable locations throughout much of the region and can be located by their call. Often heard, if not seen, in suburbs of Nairobi, in the Aberdares salient and in Ngorongoro, as well as in many parts of Malawi and Zambia.

Distribution

ORDER **Insectivora**
FAMILY **Hedgehogs** Erinaceidae

HEDGEHOG *Erinaceus albiventris*
K: Kalunguyeye   F: Herisson   D: Igel

Main colour	Length	Typical weight	Gestation period	Number of
Brown	20 cm, 8"	0.4 kg, 14 oz	35 days	young 1–9

Description
There are four species of hedgehog found in Africa but only this one species in East Africa. It is a small brown creature with an unmistakable covering of spines which envelops the entire body. The face, snout, legs and belly are bare of spines. The forehead and underparts are white, the face dark brown to black. This particular species has four toes on each foot.

Habits
Hedgehogs are mainly nocturnal and feed on insects, worms and grubs. They tend to be more visible after rains when such foods are more readily obtainable. Hedgehogs roll into a spiny ball when disturbed.

Habitat
A variety of habitats from sea-level to highland forest.

Where best seen
Widely distributed but rather local. May be heard snuffling at night especially in gardens.

Distribution

Master index to species

K = Kiswahili; F = French; D = German; L = Latin

Aardvark 178
Aardwolf 136
Abbotducker D 112
Abbot's duiker 112
Acinonyx jubatus L 144
Adenota kob L 97
Aderducker D 119
Ader's duiker 119
Aepyceros melampus 101
African civet 149
African elephant 133
African hare 184
African wild cat 148
Alcelaphus buselaphus cokii L 90
Alcelaphus buselaphus jacksonii L 90
Alcelaphus lichtensteinii L 91
Antelope musquée F 110
Aonyx capensis L 161
Atilax paludinosus L 154
Avlacode F 181
Baboon, chacma 166
Baboon, olive 166
Baboon, yellow 166
Babouin F 166
Banded mongoose 159
Bat eared fox 141
Baumschliefer D 187
Bay duiker 116
Bdeogale crassicauda L 157
Beisa oryx 88
Belette F 163
Bergriedbock D 99
Black and white colobus 172
Black backed jackal 138
Black fronted duiker 115
Black mangabey 174
Black rhinoceros 131
Blauducker D 120
Bleichböckchen D 106
Blue duiker 120
Blue monkey 167
Blue wildebeest 89
Bohor reedbuck 98
Bongo 82
Boocercus eurycerus L 82
Brazza meerkatze D 168
Breitmaulnashorn D 130
Brindled gnu 89
Bubale F 90, 91
Buffalo 78

Buffel D 78
Buffle F 78
Bunyoro rabbit 185
Burchell's zebra 129
Buschschwanzichneumon D 157
Buschschwein D 123
Bush duiker 113
Bushbaby, Demidoff's 177
Bushbaby, lesser 177
Bushbaby, thicktailed 176
Bushbuck 85
Bushpig 123
Bushy tailed mongoose 157
Bweha K 138, 139, 140
Canerat, greater 181
Canerat, lesser 181
Canis adustus L 139
Canis aureus L 140
Canis mesomelas L 138
Caracal 146
Céphalophe bai F 116
Céphalophe F 113
Céphalophe à dos jaune F 111
Céphalophe à flancs roux F 118
Céphalophe à ventre blanc F 116
Céphalophe bleu F 120
Céphalophe de Peters F 114
Céphalophe d'Abbot F 112
Céphalophe d'Ader F 119
Céphalophe rouge F 117
Cephalophus adersi L 119
Cephalophus callipygus L 114
Cephalophus dorsalis L 116
Cephalophus harveyi L 117
Cephalophus leucogaster L 116
Cephalophus monticola L 120
Cephalophus natalensis L 117
Cephalophus nigrifrons L 115
Cephalophus rubidus L 117
Cephalophus rufilatus L 118
Cephalophus spadix L 112
Cephalophus sylvicultor L 111
Ceratotherium simum L 130
Cercocebus albigena L 174
Cercocebus galeritus L 174
Cercopithecus aethiops L 170
Cercopithecus l'hoesti L 167
Cercopithecus mitis L 167
Cercopithecus neglectus L 168
Cercopithecus nictitans L 169

Cercopithèque à diademe *F* 167
Cercopithèque de Brazza *F* 168
Chacal à chabraque *F* 138
Chacal à flancs rayes *F* 139
Chacal doré *F* 140
Chacma baboon 166
Chat doré *F* 147
Chat sauvage *F* 148
Cheetah 144
Chimpanzé *F* 165
Chimpanzee 165
Choroa *K* 88
Chui *K* 143
Civette *F* 149
Civettictis civetta *L* 149
Civet, African 149
Civet, tree or palm 150
Clawless otter 161
Coke's hartebeest 90
Colobe bai *F* 173
Colobe blanc et noir *F* 172
Colobus abyssinicus *L* 172
Colobus badius *L* 173
Colobus polykomos *L* 172
Colobus, black and white 172
Colobus, red 173
Common duiker 113
Common giraffe 125
Common waterbuck 94
Common zebra 129
Connochaetes taurinus *L* 89
Crocuta crocuta *L* 134
Cynhyène *F* 137
Damaliscus hunteri *L* 93
Damaliscus lunatus *L* 92
Damalisque *F* 92
Daman de rocher *F* 186
Daman d'arbre *F* 187
Dassie 186, 187
De Brazza's monkey 168
Defassa waterbuck 94
Dendrohyrax arboreus *L* 187
Dendrohyrax dorsalis *L* 187
Dendrohyrax validus *L* 187
Derby's eland 79
Diademmeerkatze *D* 167
Diceros bicornis *L* 131
Dikdik 109
Dikdik, Guenther's 109
Dikdik, Kirk's 109
Dikidiki *K* 109
Dik-dik *F* 109
Dog, wild or hunting 137
Duiker, Abbot's 112
Duiker, Ader's 119
Duiker, bay 116

Duiker, black fronted 115
Duiker, blue 120
Duiker, bush or common 113
Duiker, Natal red 117
Duiker, Peter's 114
Duiker, red 117
Duiker, red flanked 118
Duiker, Ruwenzori red 117
Duiker, white bellied 116
Duiker, yellow backed 111
Duiker, Zanzibar 119
Duma *K* 144
Dwarf mongoose 160
Eastern lowland gorilla 164
Ecureuil foisseur *F* 182
Elan *F* 79
Elanantilope *D* 79
Eland 79
Eland, Derby's 79
Eléphant *F* 133
Elephant, African 133
Ensumu *K* 97
Equus burchelli *L* 129
Equus grevyi *L* 128
Erdferkel *D* 178
Erdhörnchen *D* 182
Erdwolf *D* 136
Erinaceus albiventris *L* 188
Erythrocebus patas *L* 171
Falbkatze *D* 148
Felis aurata *L* 147
Felis caracal *L* 146
Felis lybica *L* 148
Felis serval *L* 145
Fingerotter *D* 161
Fisi *K* 134, 135
Fisi maji *K* 161
Fisi ndogo *K* 136
Fleckenhalsotter *D* 161
Fleckenhyäne *D* 134
Fourmillier *F* 178
Fox, bat eared 141
Fringe eared oryx 88
Fungo *K* 149
Funo *K* 107, 108, 117, 118
Galago à queue épaissé *F* 176
Galago crassicaudatus *L* 176
Galago de Senegal *F* 177
Galago senegalensis *L* 177
Galago 176, 177
Galerella sanguinea *L* 158
Gazella grantii *L* 103
Gazella thomsonii *L* 104
Gazelle de Grant *F* 103
Gazelle de Thomson *F* 104
Gazelle de Waller *F* 102

Gazelle, Grant's 103
Gazelle, Thomson's 104
Gemeine riedbock *D* 98
Genetta genetta *L* 151
Genetta tigrina *L* 151
Genette *F* 151
Genet, large spotted 151
Genet, small spotted 151
Gepard *D* 144
Gerenuk 102
Giant forest hog 121
Ginsterkatze *D* 151
Giraffa camelopardalis *L* 125
Giraffa camelopardalis reticulata *L* 126
Giraffe 125, 126
Giraffengazelle *D* 102
Giraffe, common or Masai 125
Giraffe, reticulated 126
Giraffe, Rothschild's 126
Gnou *F* 89
Gnu 89
Gnu, brindled 89
Gnu, white bearded 89
Golden cat 147
Golden jackal 140
Golden monkey 167
Goldkatze *D* 147
Goldschakal *D* 140
Gorilla 164
Gorilla gorilla *L* 164
Gorilla, eastern lowland 164
Gorilla, mountain 164
Gorille *F* 164
Grantgazelle *D* 103
Grant's gazelle 103
Grasantilope *D* 97
Gras-hase *D* 185
Greater canerat 181
Greater kudu 80
Greiichneumon *D* 153
Grevyzebra *D* 128
Grevy's zebra 128
Grey duiker 113
Grivet *F* 170
Grosschimpanse *D* 165
Grosselefant *D* 133
Grossflusspferd *D* 124
Grossriedbock *D* 100
Ground squirrel 182
Grünmeerkatze *D* 170
Grysbok de Sharpe *F* 108
Grysbok, Sharpe's 108
Guenther's dikdik 109
Guepard *F* 144
Guib harnaché *F* 85
Hare, African 184

Hare, scrub 184
Hartebeest, Coke's 90
Hartebeest, Hunter's 93
Hartebeest, Jackson's 90
Hartebeest, Lichtenstein's 91
Hase *D* 184
Hedgehog 188
Helogale parvula *L* 160
Herisson *F* 188
Herpestes ichneumon *L* 153
Heterohyrax brucei *L* 186
Hippopotame *F* 124
Hippopotamus 124
Hippopotamus amphibius *L* 124
Hippotrague *F* 86
Hippotrague noir *F* 87
Hippotragus equinus *L* 86
Hippotragus niger *L* 87
Hirola 93
Hocheur *F* 169
Hog, giant forest 121
Honey badger 162
Hönigdachs *D* 162
Hook lipped rhinoceros 131
Hunting dog 137
Husaraffe *D* 171
Hyaena hyaena *L* 135
Hyänenhund *D* 137
Hyena, spotted 134
Hyena, striped 135
Hyène rayée *F* 135
Hyène tachetée *F* 134
Hylochère géant *F* 121
Hylochoerus meinertzhageni *L* 121
Hyrax, rock 186
Hyrax, tree 187
Hystrix africae-australis *L* 180
Hystrix cristata *L* 180
Ichneumia albicauda *L* 152
Ictonyx striatus *L* 163
Igel *D* 188
Impala 101
Jackal, black backed 138
Jackal, golden 140
Jackal, side striped 139
Jackson's hartebeest 90
Kakukuona *K* 179
Kalunguyeye *K* 188
Kamendegere *K* 183
Kanu *K* 151
Kiboko *K* 124
Kichachu *K* 115
Kicheche *K* 163
Kifaru *K* 130, 131
Kima *K* 167
Kindi *K* 182

191

Kindiri *K* 182
Kipoke *K* 111
Kirk's dikdik 109
Kitafe *K* 166
Klein kudu *D* 81
Klipschliefer *D* 186
Klipspringer 105
Kob 94
Kob de Buffon *F* 97
Kob lechwe *F* 95
Kobus ellipsiprymnus defassa *L*
Kobus ellipsiprymnus ellipsiprymnus *L*
Kobus lechwe *L* 95
Kobus vardonii *L* 97
Kob, Uganda 97
Komba *K* 177
Kongoni 90, 91
Korongo *K* 86
Koudou *F* 80
Kronenducker *D* 118
Kudu, greater 80
Kudu, lesser 81
Kuhantilope *D* 90, 91
Kuru *K* 94
Lapin sauvage *F* 185
Large grey mongoose 153
Large spotted genet 151
Lechwe 95
Leier *D* 92
Leopard 143
Lepus capensis *L* 184
Lepus saxatilis *L* 184
Lesser bushbaby 177
Lesser canerat 181
Lesser kudu 81
Lichtenstein's hartebeest 91
Lièvre *F* 184
Lièvre sauteur *F* 183
Lion 142
Litocranius walleri *L* 102
Litschi *D* 95
Loffelhund *D* 141
Loutre à cou tacheté *F* 161
Loutre à joues blanches *F* 161
Löwe *D* 142
Loxodonta africana *L* 133
Lutra maculicollis *L* 161
Lycaon pictus *L* 137
L'Hoest's monkey
Madoqua guentheri *L* 109
Madoqua kirkii *L* 109
Makaku *K* 164
Mangabé noir *F* 174
Mangabey, black 174
Mangouste à queue blanche *F* 152

Mangouste à queue touffue *F* 157
Mangouste de Meller *F* 155
Mangouste de Selous *F* 156
Mangouste des marais *F* 154
Mangouste grise *F* 153
Mangouste nain *F* 160
Mangouste rayeé *F* 159
Mangouste rouge *F* 158
Manis gigantea *L* 179
Manis temminckii *L* 179
Marsh mongoose 154
Mauswiesel *D* 163
Mbega *K* 172
Mbogo *K* 78
Mbuzi mawe *K* 105
Mbwa mwitu *K* 137
Mellermaushund *D* 155
Meller's mongoose 155
Mellivora capensis *L* 162
Mondo *K* 145
Mongoose, banded 159
Mongoose, bushy tailed 157
Mongoose, dwarf 160
Mongoose, large grey 153
Mongoose, marsh or water 154
Mongoose, Meller's 155
Mongoose, Selous' 156
Mongoose, slender 158
Mongoose, white tailed 152
Monkey, black and white colobus 172
Monkey, blue 167
Monkey, De Brazza's 168
Monkey, golden 167
Monkey, L'Hoest's 167
Monkey, patas 171
Monkey, red colobus 173
Monkey, red tailed 169
Monkey, samango 167
Monkey, Sykes' 167
Monkey, vervet 170
Monkey, white nosed 169
Moschusböckchen *D* 110
Mountain gorilla 164
Mountain reedbuck 99
Muhanga *K* 178
Mungos mungo *L* 159
Nandinia binotata *L* 150
Nandinie *F* 150
Natal red duiker 117
Ndezi *K* 181
Ndimba *K* 120
Ndongoro *K* 82
Ndovu *K* 133
Neotragus batesi *L* 110
Neotragus moschatus *L* 110
Ngiri *K* 122

Nguchiro *K* 152, 153, 154, 155, 156, 157, 158, 159
Nguruwe *K* 121, 123
Nsya *K* 113
Nunga *K* 119
Nungu *K* 180
Nyala 83
Nyamera *K* 92
Nyani *K* 166
Nyati *K* 78
Nyegere *K* 162
Nyumbu *K* 89
Nzohe *K* 84
Okapi 127
Okapia johnstoni *L* 127
Olive baboon 166
Oréotrague *F* 105
Oreotragus oreotragus *L* 105
Oribi 106
Orycteropus afer *L* 178
Oryx 88
Oryx gazella *L* 88
Oryx, beisa 88
Oryx, fringe eared 88
Otocyon *F* 141
Otocyon megalotis *L* 141
Otter, clawless 161
Otter, spotted necked 161
Ourebia ourebi *L* 106
Ourébie *F* 106
Paa *K* 110, 120
Paka pori *K* 148
Pala hala *K* 87
Pallah *F* 101
Pan troglodytes *L* 165
Pangolin 179
Panthera leo *L* 142
Panthera pardus *L* 143
Panthère *F* 143
Papio anubis *L* 166
Papio cynocephalus *L* 166
Papio ursinus *L* 166
Paracynictis selousi *L* 156
Pardelroller *D* 150
Patas monkey 171
Pavian *D* 166
Pedetes capensis *L* 183
Pembere *K* 187
Perodicticus potto *L* 175
Petersducker *D* 114
Peter's Duiker 114
Petit koudou *F* 81
Pferdeantilope *D* 86
Phacochère *F* 122
Phacochoerus aethiopicus *L* 122
Pigmy antelope 110
Pimbi *K* 186
Poecilogale albinucha *L* 163
Pofu *K* 79
Polecat, striped 163
Pongo *K* 85
Porcupine 180
Porc-épique *F* 180
Potamochère *F* 123
Potamochoerus porcus *L* 123
Potto 175
Procavia johnstoni *L* 186
Procavia habessinica *L* 186
Pronolagus marjorita *L* 185
Pronolagus rupestris *L* 185
Protèle *F* 136
Proteles cristatus *L* 136
Puku 96
Punda milia *K* 129
Rabbit, Bunyoro 185
Rabbit, red rock 185
Raphicerus campestris *L* 107
Raphicerus sharpei *L* 108
Rappenantilope *D* 87
Ratel 162
Red colobus 173
Red duiker 117
Red flanked duiker 118
Red rock rabbit 185
Red tailed monkey 169
Redunca *F* 98
Redunca arundinum *L* 100
Redunca de montagne *F* 99
Redunca fulvorufula *L* 99
Redunca grande *F* 100
Redunca redunca *L* 98
Reedbuck, bohor 98
Reedbuck, mountain 99
Reedbuck, southern 100
Rhinoceros blanc *F* 130
Rhinoceros noir *F* 131
Rhinoceros, black or hook lipped 131
Rhinoceros, white or square lipped 130
Rhynchogale melleri 155
Riesenducker *D* 111
Riesengalago *D* 176
Roan antelope 86
Rock hyrax 186
Rohrratte *D* 181
Rotducker *D* 117
Roter stummelaffe *D* 173
Rotflankenducker *D* 118
Rotichneumon *D* 158
Ruwenzori red duiker 117
Sable antelope 87
Samango monkey 167
Schabrackenschakal *D* 138

Schirrantilope *D* 85
Schopfemangabe *D* 174
Schuppentier *D* 179
Schwarztfersenantilope *D* 101
Schwarzruckenducker *D* 116
Scrub hare 184
Selousmaushund *D* 156
Selous' mongoose 156
Serval 145
Servalkatze *D* 145
Sharpe greisbock *D* 108
Sharpe's grysbok 108
Side striped jackal 139
Simba *K* 142
Simba mangu *K* 146
Singe rouge *F* 171
Sitatunga 84
Slender mongoose 158
Small spotted genet 151
Soko *K* 165
Southern reedbuck 100
Spiessbock *D* 88
Spitzmaulnashorn *D* 131
Spotted hyena 134
Spotted necked otter 161
Springhare 183
Springhase *D* 183
Square lipped rhinceros 130
Squirrel, ground 182
Stachelschwein *D* 180
Steenbok 107
Steinböckchen *D* 107
Steppengalago *D* 177
Steppenzebra *D* 129
Streifenhyäne *D* 135
Streifenschakal *D* 139
Strepsiceros imberbis *L* 81
Striped hyena 135
Striped polecat 163
Striped weasel 163
Sumpfantilope *D* 84
Sumpfichneumon *D* 154
Sungura *K* 184
Suni 110
Swala granti *K* 103
Swala pala *K* 101
Swala tomi *K* 104
Swala twiga *K* 102
Sykes' monkey 167
Sylvicapra grimmia *L* 113
Syncerus caffer *L* 78
Tandala *K* 80
Tandala ndogo *K* 81
Taurotragus derbianus *L* 79
Taurotragus oryx *L* 79
Taya *K* 106

Tembo *K* 133
Thick tailed bushbaby 176
Thomsongazelle *D* 104
Thomson's gazelle 104
Thornicroft's giraffe 125
Thryonomys gregorianus *L* 181
Thryonomys swinderianus *L* 181
Tieflandnyala *D* 83
Tohe *K* 98
Tohe ya kusina *K* 100
Tohe ya milima *K* 99
Tondoro *K* 107
Topi 92
Tragelaphus angasii *L* 83
Tragelaphus scriptus *L* 85
Tragelaphus spekei *L* 84
Tragelaphus strepsiceros *L* 80
Tree civet 150
Tree hyrax 187
Tsessebe 92
Tumbili *K* 170
Twiga *K* 125, 126
Vervet monkey 170
Waldschwein *D* 121
Warthog 122
Warzenschwein *D* 122
Wasserbock *D* 94
Water mongoose 154
Waterbuck, common or ringed 94
Waterbuck, Defassa 94
Weasel, striped 163
Weissbartstumelaffe *D* 172
Weissbauchducker *D* 116
Weissnase *D* 169
Weissschwanzichneumon *D* 152
White bellied duiker 116
White nosed monkey 169
White rhinoceros 130
White tailed mongoose 152
Wild cat, African 148
Wild dog 137
Wildebeest 89
Wüstenluchs *D* 146
Xerus erythropus *L* 182
Xerus rutilus *L* 182
Yellow baboon 166
Yellow backed duiker 111
Zanzibar duiker 119
Zebra manguste *D* 159
Zebra, common or Burchell's 129
Zebra, Grevy's 128
Zèbre de Grevy *F* 128
Zèbre de steppe *F* 129
Zibetkatze *D* 149
Zorilla, Zorille *F* 163
Zwergichneumon *D* 160